Your Personality Drives You

Your Personality Drives You

Dan Jankowski

Author/Publisher's Note: This publication is designed to provide accurate information in regard to the subject material within. It is sold with the understanding that the publisher/author is not engaged in providing legal, medical, psychological, or other professional service. If expert counseling or psychological assistance is required, the services of a competent professional should be sought.

Library of Congress Cataloging-in-Publication Data
    Jankowski, Dan
    Your Personality Drives You

ISBN-13: 978-1456378066
ISBN-10: 1456378066

~~Dedicated to my siblings, Sonny and Marianne

Contents

Acknowledgements

I extend my appreciation to the many participants who provided the necessary data to make this research possible. I am also indebted to Julio Garulo Muñoz for meticulously correlating the required data. Lastly, I am especially grateful to Donna Baker for her ever-present encouragement and fullest support throughout the course of this book.

Preface

We do it virtually every day. For the typical American, it is as natural as breathing and eating. We refer, of course, to driving. Yet, we may wonder what influences us to behave the way we do when we get into a hundred cubic foot compartment mounted on a steel chassis. Why do we act the way we do when getting behind the wheel? *Your Personality Drives You* specifically addresses these issues in discussing eight personality patterns that functionally "drive" you to find expression on the road. As each of us has a dominant style, having blended traits in more than one pattern commonly defines a personality pattern. It is this uniquely blended pattern of personality that influences our driving behavior.

All of us do battle with our dark sides, or the *shadow,* as discussed in Jungian terms, particularly when our defense mechanisms are activated under acute conditions of stress. Ever wonder what makes you vulnerable to unpredictable behavioral and emotional challenges—yours as well as others? At times there is a fine line regarding normalcy and *ab*-normalcy, as we may find ourselves "snapping" at another motorist. One necessarily asks, "Who are the normal drivers? Even if identified, do they always drive normally? What do they look like?" Normal adaptive personalities, to be sure, experience "transformations," as vividly portrayed in Robert Louis Stevenson's classic, the *Strange Case of Dr. Jekyll and Mr. Hyde.* To maintain a semblance of normalcy we habitually show our Dr. Jekyll faces to the world. This is our *persona,* a Latin term derived from the theatrical masks worn by ancient actors. It is specifically this amenable, Jekyll side of ourselves we wish others to see and like. Nevertheless, on occasion, the "Hyde" character, or *shadow* emerges. It is this dark side of ourselves we wish to hide from public view. The *shadow,* however, finds expression in everyone and unexpectedly surfaces when overwhelmed by stress.

Stevenson's vivid characterization of Mr. Hyde—a character we find ourselves occasionally imitating behind the wheel—confounds the Jekyll in all of us. Stevenson portrays Jekyll as a responsible, considerate, and accommodating person much of the time, unlike the hidden *shadow* in Hyde's cruel, indifferent, and self-centered demeanor that surreptitiously engulfs the sensitive nature of Jekyll. Stevenson's analysis is true for all of us—on and off the road. Under times of extreme stress, this transformation causes us to become emotionally conflicted. In discussing individual personality, we will examine Stevenson's characters to uncover the "hidden Hyde" as we get behind the wheel and react abnormally, particularly when other drivers violate our personal space.

Almost every driver has been cut off in traffic at one time or another. This example is just one of the many ways others deprive us of personal space on the road. During highway construction, for instance, a right lane closure often becomes a game to see how many drivers can pass you while you remain merged in the left lane. The "intruders" quickly dart toward the construction cordon squeezing determinedly in front of you. The degree and intensity of the anger you feel distinguishes one driver's irritability from another's rage in such a situation. How we react to such a violation of personal space is what makes the difference and is largely contingent on one's personality style. Personality varies, as does the make of a vehicle. Ultimately, personality style will dictate one's aggressive tendencies on the road—surreptitiously uncovering the "hidden Hyde" behind the persona.

This book is not simply about road rage. Rather, its unique approach invites us to discover our true personality that essentially drives us while behind the wheel. *Your Personality Drives You* systematically, statistically, and at times humorously examines the various patterns of driving behavior.

People are normally drawn to self-help books for discovery. This book will hopefully provide that "aha" moment by identifying the personality style that drives you on the road. The data for *Your Personality Drives You* is derived from more than five hundred independent surveys compiled across all age groups and correlated with the

Emotions Profile Index.[1] Its ten chapters focus on eight personality styles in defining associated driving behaviors. How one interacts with the environment, what model and color of vehicle one drives, how one expresses anger and copes with stress are features that vary with personality. The stage is set, and you are invited to come along for the ride. Discover within the following chapters how your personality style "drives" you.

Your Personality Drives You

❶ Driving Is Revealing

As Shakespeare reminds us in *As You Like It,* "All the world's a stage, and all the men and women merely players. They have their exits and their entrances, and one person in his time plays many parts...." Some of us play an actor consumed with anger or one who is guided by equanimity. Some act out of compliance, while others know only fear. Our roles essentially are set, revealing the story of our life's performance. All people exhibit some form of theatrical presentation, dancing to the beat of different drummers. Yet, when on stage, we often dance and act differently.

Nowhere do we play out our roles more prominently than in our performances on the nation's highways. For it is on the road, where we usually take off our masks, the *persona,* as coined by ancient Latin and Greek actors. Undeniably, driving reveals our predictable performance—it is where more than any other place, that our true selves play out who we actually are. Moreover, perhaps because of anonymity, it is on these roads where our authentic selves find expression and true lines are loudly spoken. On this stage, actors from varied lifestyles concomitantly play out their authentic roles. All of us have a leading role, acting it out in our vehicles. Some act to the delight of some and to the chagrin of others. A number of drivers are heroes, keeping others from harm. Others are villains, threatening the lives of many. Yet, there are those who are timid and apprehensive, at times, forgetful of their lines and distracted by other "players." One's role, acted out on our nation's highways, is expressed through a dynamic script, with characters fashioned predictably by each actor. Dramatic characteristics naturally find meaning in distinct individual personality, driving us in our roles.

If we want to know the true personality of others, simply observe how they drive. How a person drives an automobile conveys a clear and transparent uniqueness, acting out a distinctive pattern that differs from one driver to the next. Certainly, all people mechanically operate the vehicle similarly, although with varied levels of skill. However, the true performance rests in the temperament of the individual steering the vehicle, and essentially varies with each driver. The way an individual drives is singularly distinct—a pattern of traits, behaviors, attitudes, and emotions uniquely mirroring one's personality style. Plainly stated, driving is revealing, disclosing one's authentic character. Nevertheless, why do people drive the way they do, playing different roles? Very simply, with the anonymity the driver enjoys, the road becomes the stage on which our hidden parts are revealed. Yet, this enigmatic question begs more questions. Why do some people buy sports cars and others light trucks? Why do some drivers pass every vehicle they possibly can on the highway, while others fear merging onto the expressway? Each of us, though biologically very similar, is actually very dissimilar psychologically. The way one interacts with the highway environment, particularly in expressing anger and coping with stress, is essentially a function of one's unique personality. An awareness of our personality behind the wheel can bring us closer to the seemingly elusive answer.

Our driving personalities define who we really are. Individual personalities vary behind the wheel as much as the models of the vehicles driven on the road today. If we want to know what others are really like, watch the signs— no, not the signs on the road—watch how others behave behind the wheel. Observe the cues. Some are tense, anxious, and indecisive. Others are compulsive, unable to deviate from rigid habits. The apprehensive and timid drivers, fearful of traffic, are reluctant to take even the slightest of risks. Yet, others are forceful, if not violent, racing to steal the lead. Thankfully, though, a goodly number remains civil. On the road, even more so than on the stage of life, we act out our true personality traits that direct our thinking, behaviors, and emotions—our entire being. Drivers literally and figuratively bring their personalities to the road, and particularly under the guise of anonymity, reveal their true, underlying character.

As in life, each personality reacts differently to the stressors on the road. Some personalities by their very nature are forceful and hostile, yet others are friendly and cooperative. As in the animal kingdom, lions and tigers respond with forcefulness, while rabbits and deer withdraw with timidity. Similarly, in the face of conflict and frustration, some individuals strike out forcefully and others apprehensively withdraw. Certainly not all drivers are disposed to aggressiveness, though some individuals, nonetheless, have a greater propensity than others. Each of us manages anger and stress differently and responds accordingly. For many, muttering a few words behind the wheel is quite natural and a normal instinctive reaction to anger. Lashing out against another driver, sometimes uncontrollably, is not. A number of personalities, much like the lions and tigers, are forceful by their very nature and are naturally more prone to react aggressively toward another. Fortunately, though, scores of drivers adaptively manage their stress on the road and respond appropriately.

Distracting Anxiety

Distractions ebb and flow. When behind the wheel, do you consciously drive your car, or are you on autopilot, with a flood of distractions occupying your mind? According to the National Highway Traffic Association (NHTSA), 10% of all fatal collisions involve some form of driver distraction.[2] Drivers are distracted both externally as well as internally. External distractions while numerous are easily recognized. They range from navigating wintry weather to using a cell phone. Manufacturers develop safety features, such as hands-free audio and visual equipment, sensor warnings, and electronic stability control to reduce distractions. Though these advanced sensor systems might serve to lessen the external overload, they can seemingly become distractions in and of themselves. Nevertheless, these safety features, to some degree, minimize external distractions.

Internal distractions, however, are infinitely more difficult to reduce than external disturbances. Internal distractions are unwanted thoughts that can cause worry, fear, self-doubt, and physiological symptoms, such as sweaty palms, headache, or a queasy stomach. Essentially, we experience cognitive dissonance and remain conflicted until the unease can be resolved. The dissonance overloads the mind, with rational and irrational beliefs competing for our attention. Internal distractions, perhaps more than external distractions, will readily impair performance on the road. Internal interference results in an inability to focus on the task at hand, jeopardizing safety and lowering reaction time. Internal "noise" reduction involves identifying the nature of the distraction, then finding methods to clear the mind for driving. When the noise volume increases, simply dial it down. Minimize the interference by regaining focus. Utilize a brief relaxation technique, such as deep breathing, to soothe the mind. Internally we are constantly "spammed" with needless thoughts, generating negative emotion. How one drives on the public stage is largely related to one's ability to control not only the vehicle, but also one's thoughts, impulses, and behaviors. Some stress responses are so subtle that we are not even aware of them. All of us have an optimal stress level, though, with the continuous pressure of road stressors, we can easily reach a state of distress. Sustained negative affect is an important measure for one's discharge of anger and the "fuel," which fans the raging flames. As we become distressed, internal adaptive systems necessary to maintain equilibrium become unbalanced. Internal distractions, increased by the driver's distressing thoughts and negative emotion, can nevertheless be lessened by simply distracting the unwanted distractions. When distress is resolved, homeostatic balance returns.

Distractions, though, whether external or internal, impede the necessary attention and reaction time, and play a part in 25% of motor vehicle accidents.[3] Ultimately, stress increases, consuming the driver's mental energy. All of us have different concerns, worries, or fears and react differently to road stressors. For example, one's impatient sounding of the horn, timed precisely as the arrow turns green in the left turning lane, may be perceived as a minor irritant to some drivers and perhaps elicit a sigh. As the tolerant driver sensibly ignores it, the incident is quickly dismissed. Yet, for another, the same toot of the horn might be the cue that summons distressing anxiety or even anger. On one end of the spectrum, the distracting toot can be a minor annoyance quickly forgotten, while on the other, its impact is long lasting. A driver's reaction to road distraction inevitably varies with the ability to control its interference.

Unlike external distractions, *only you* create internal distractions and it is solely within *your* power to reduce and manage the internal noise. With the record number of automobiles on our roads today, congestion on our streets and highways has created more of an emotional challenge than many drivers can psychically manage. Imagine, for example, driving bumper-to-bumper on a steamy summer afternoon. Your car is barely crawling when a construction zone appears, suddenly reducing the 55-mph speed limit. The three-lane expressway soon compresses into two. You feel nauseous from the exhaust fumes of other cars that surround you. Under such circumstances, tempers normally become increasingly hot—and then it happens. A motorist riding on the shoulder of the road roars past your car and tries to creep in front of you. You think to yourself, "I will not let this intruder in," as you narrow the gap, literally by inches, to prevent the vehicle from cutting in. You make your decision not to let the intrusive driver in front of you. Assorted muscles then become tense throughout your body, involuntarily and almost instantaneously reacting to this intrusion. What you think and feel will assuredly affect how you react. To gain greater control of your actions, you learn to adaptively manage your internal distractions. Your personality style, to be sure, will dictate the degree and intensity of the internal distraction, as well as your reaction.

Learn Your Stressors

Stress is as common today as the seemingly endless miles of the nation's highways. Typically, the adaptive normal experience of stress is fleeting and short-lived, while the maladaptive, abnormal experience is enduring and pervasive. It is as noxious as the air we breathe. Stress, to be sure, is a normal human response, and its physiological

9

and psychological effects can startle, stimulate, perplex, endanger, or aggravate the biological system. Have you ever been on a highway at night when suddenly behind you looms a vehicle with its high beams shining directly into your rearview mirror? At first, you just hope the motorist passes you. As you decrease your speed, your tolerance level weakens as the reflection becomes increasingly blinding with each passing mile-marker. Your stress response further elevates, preparing the body for "fight or flight." Perhaps after uttering a few choice expletives to yourself, thoughts of retaliation creep into your mind, as your stress level elevates proportionately to your blood pressure. To resolve the predicament, you may slow down, tap the brake lights, or speed ahead, all seemingly to no avail. Frustration and varied degrees of anger likely mount with the continuous glare of the irritating headlights. The body's complex natural alarm system is engaged, releasing stress hormones, to include adrenaline and cortisol, leaving you tense, irritable, and short-tempered. Moreover, how would you react to the above situation following an irritable day at the office, or after a quarrel with your spouse? Your stress alarm is already activated, and you are likely stressed before hitting the road. What prevents you from acting out? How can you control underlying urges? Curbing stress requires managing your thoughts, behaviors, and environment. Only gaining control over stressful events will eventually return the biological system to its homeostatic balance.

All stressors seem magnified in the driver's seat. Learning to recognize your particular stressors on the road will help curb anxiety. Once the stressors are identified, the brakes need to be applied. Susceptibility is a by-product of chronic stress, with some personalities more vulnerable to its effects. Negativity creeps into the mind, and one's normal controls seemingly become unhinged. Too often, the inner demons emerge, and as a result, control is lost. With respect to control, consider an occasion when you might have experienced a sudden outburst of rage that seemed to overwhelm you. You quickly catch yourself, but ask perplexedly, "Why did I do that?" To understand the answer, we must realize that all of us wage war with our hidden parts, or the *shadow,* as Carl Jung described, mainly when our coping mechanisms are tested under stringent conditions of stress. At times, there exists a fine line with regard to normalcy and *ab*-normalcy. Determining which individuals drive adaptively and which drive *mal*-adaptively cannot always be observed with certainty. One necessarily asks, "Who is the normal, adaptive driver? What does he or she look like? And even if normal drivers can be identified, could there be any assurance that they will always drive adaptively?" Most adaptive personalities also experience "transformations," as artfully depicted in Stevenson's account of the *Strange Case of Dr. Jekyll and Mr. Hyde.* Most people, though, readily present their Jekyll faces, or *persona*, much of the time. The *persona* is the side that we want others to like, the image we wish to present to the

11

public. Yet, we often wear more than one mask, much like the chameleon that changes to suit the situational stage. An internal struggle ensues between the good *persona* and evil *shadow*. Failing to accept and control the *shadow* part of ourselves results in the projection of unwanted malice onto others. Unfortunately, there are times when the hidden part, or *shadow*, finds dramatic expression in the normal adaptive personality. The following story illustrates this transformation, even by an officer sworn to uphold the law.

A local police officer was suspended today for allegedly spraying Mace at a driver and his 5-year-old son during a traffic dispute.

The officer was off-duty and driving his own car but still in uniform during an incident. He also faces an assault charge in criminal court, and he was ordered to get counseling for anger management.

He has been suspended for three weeks, said the manager for employee relations in Jefferson County's personnel division. He could appeal the punishment to the personnel board, which has the power to revise the penalty.

We tell employees, "Be careful what you ask for."

The officer and another motorist of Springville got into an altercation on Interstate 59 in neighboring St. Claire County. The motorist allegedly made an obscene gesture when the officer attempted to pull him over, and both men got out of their cars at an exit.

In a ruling ordering the suspension, the officer admitted becoming angry because the motorist was driving slowly in the fast lane, and that he sprayed the other man with Mace.

Both drivers filed criminal complaints. [4]

Stevenson's characterization of the "hidden Hyde," a character we find ourselves all too often imitating behind the wheel, confounds the Jekyll in us, particularly during times of undue stress. Though we prefer to see ourselves as Jekyll, demonstrating responsible, caring, and courteous behavior much of the time, Hyde's cruel, unsympathetic and self-centered behaviors, on occasion, surreptitiously overwhelm the adaptive nature in everyone. Stevenson not only stresses that there is a "hidden Hyde" in all of us, but also notes that it is actually hidden much deeper in those unaware of its presence. Jekyll could not easily reject the evil part of himself, though he struggled to do so. When he looked in the mirror as Hyde, he was unable to see the grotesque figure others saw because he failed to become familiar with his own dark side. A wife might comment, for example, that her husband transforms from a Dr. Jekyll to a Mr. Hyde when he gets behind the wheel of a car. Most often he fails to see the obvious change or perhaps accept it. Too often transformation occurs without awareness.

Masks are removed, at times unknowingly, in response to the anonymity of the road. Hidden anger, likely compounded by stressors of everyday life, emerges. Suppressed anger quickly surfaces and tempers ignite, with both Jekyll and Hyde struggling to gain control of impulses. A personal experience clearly illustrates this struggle.

> As I was waiting at a red light one morning, and the light was about to turn green, the driver behind me in an SUV "tapped" my bumper. After inspecting

the bumper, I determined that there was no damage and was about to be on my way with a conciliatory wave. But suddenly, I heard the SUV driver shout in my direction, "Why did *you* back into me?"

At this point, his words of accusation left me "clearly seeing red" and shaking my head in disbelief hearing this brazen driver's argumentative remark. Since there was no damage, I took the prudent course and returned to my car, thinking, "Discretion is the better part of valor."

The license plate told the story. It read *DEWARS1*.

Thus it is with all of us—both on and off the road. Without warning, and often without our conscious awareness, instincts overwhelm us. The "hidden Hyde" is uncovered in all of us. Anger, likely compounded by stressors carried from our personal life, is particularly evident when we become "unhinged" behind the wheel.

Stretching a rubber band beyond its tension limits will eventually cause it to snap. You may lose emotional control and just like the rubber band, eventually snap when tension expands beyond the breaking point. How you react, though, is a reflection of your personality style. You may be doing more harm to your body than you think if you let stress get the best of you. Inevitably, you begin to hear the knocks, as your biological warning light goes on.

As technological sensors serve to reduce external distraction and increase road safety, our emotional feelers can similarly lessen our internal distractions. Reduce internal distractions through clearing your mind. Introduce driver-friendly thoughts into your inner driving vocabulary. Distract distress through self-soothing techniques found in the following chapters. Fortunately, less than 15% of the respondents acknowledged that they remain upset following an irritable occurrence on the road. Sustained negative affect is an important measure for one's discharge of anger. While the vast majority of motorists may experience irritation on the road, it is, for the most part, fleeting. Though road rage is a problem on our roadways, the good news for many motorists is that aside from an occasional "Jekyll and Hyde" transformation, sustained irritation appears relatively low among the average driving public. Yet, as the number of drivers and automobiles increase in future years, this percentage may certainly rise.

In Summary

Why, then, do people drive the way they do? Though the answer may seem elusive, the following chapters will shed light on this question. Our personality patterns are structurally defined, and unlike the weather, do not readily change. If you were forceful in school and currently display *type-A* characteristics as an adult, you are likely an assertive driver on the road. Or, alternatively, if you grew up a shy youngster, you may resemble a timid driver on the road. Our personalities develop an embedded, essential form at an early age and do not measurably change as maturity extends into adulthood. Some easily adapt to the expectations of adulthood, while others seem ill-equipped.

As with the vehicles we drive, each of us varies in personality, playing different roles in life. We perceive the environment differently, acting out our dramas individually on varied stages. An impulsive personality, for example, will react quite differently to the "rules of the road" than a conscientious personality. An aggressive personality, though, will likely intimidate those in his or her path. Our personality determines how we act, how we think, how we feel, and, of course, how we drive. Can we apply personality criteria to our driving behaviors? Do individual styles of personality drive differently? Are some styles more assertive or timid than others?

On our journey to understand the answers to these questions, we shall examine eight personality styles derived from the *Emotions Profile Index* [5] in relation to driving behaviors, choice of vehicles, and among other things, propensity for rage on the road. Driving is very telling. It identifies who we are, oftentimes without our conscious realization. During this journey of discovery, hopefully we will also gain an appreciation of other motorists' personality styles, as well as recognize which personality really drives us on the road. Script in hand, we are ready to view the characters in their respective roles. Let's now steer our way through these revealing personality patterns and consciously unveil our driving "masks" in the process. In the following chapters, let's recognize our personality styles and discover what truly influences us to behave the way we do behind the wheel.

❷ The Conscientious Pattern

When considering the conscientious personality, watch for the "signs," so to speak, which indicate compliance behind the wheel. Strict observance of the "rules of the road" clearly distinguishes this personality. The following identifying characteristics describe this pattern.

- Thorough in all activities

- Meticulously maintains personal vehicle

- Scrupulously obeys the rules of the road

- Always aware of other motorists

- Believes tried-and-true methods are the best way of doing something

- Becomes lost on unfamiliar roads

- Takes pride in being a careful and skilled driver

- Plans and organizes the route to be traveled

- Regularly maintains recommended distance between vehicles on the road

- Feels tense and apprehensive when approaching hazardous situations

- Overly self-critical at times

- Prone to rationalization

Extremely conscientious and diligent about their driving habits, as with every facet of their lives, details are carefully considered and planned. Even the smallest of decisions are heavily weighed, from the route selected to the measured interval they must maintain between cars. Rarely do these individuals leave anything to chance. Disciplined in their driving behavior and obedient in their strict adherence to the regulations, the conscientious driver attentively respects the rules of the road and expects other motorists to do the same. The conscientious driver is careful, reserved, and law-abiding, one who would not typically take chances, nor jeopardize the safety of others.

These individuals obey the rules at all times. They observe *no left turn* signs at an intersection, *no passing* signs around curves, and posted speed limits to ensure safety, but even more so because it is the law and its observance thought to be necessary to preserve order on the road. They strive for propriety on the road and rely on the rules, not only out of external compliance to the law, but also because compliance to external regulations helps reduce personal ambiguity. For this style, compliance helps soothe their internal need for order. Since these individuals normally adopt a rigid observance of the rules, they can become, at times, adamant in their actions toward others who ignore the regulations. They scrupulously follow the law, not necessarily focusing on the spirit, but rather its letter. You may have observed such individuals driving next to you on the road, for example, those who set their cruise control to the exact speed limit posted, while musing, "What's the big hurry? We'll get there and we'll get there safely." Though unquestionably respectful of other motorists, on occasion, their tolerance is tested, particularly when others scoff at the laws. At such times, these drivers may become all the more determined to maintain order on the road, so much so that they may even attempt to "enforce" the law themselves by doggedly maintaining the speed limit—even in the passing lane.

More often than not, these individuals drive at or near the posted speed limit. From time to time, they may be found in the left lane leading a small cortege of very disgruntled motorists who are anxiously waiting to pass. When conscientious motorists rationalize to themselves that expressway traffic is moving too quickly they may unconsciously attempt to control it. Though, it is difficult to determine if such individuals are truly obeying the laws or if they are just implicitly imposing their strictures upon other drivers by "insisting" that they also comply with the posted speed limit.

When the rules seem too uncertain or ambiguous, however, these individuals might become constricted, experiencing increased anxiety. Under extremely demanding pressure, they can become inflexible, which in turn clouds their decisions. Consequently, they are typically wanting when quick reaction time, or split-second decision-making abilities, is so often necessary on the roads today. When they become anxious, for example, in locating an unfamiliar exit or encountering a confusing road condition, a moment of indecision may arise. Normally, though, these individuals are in complete control of themselves, and their vehicles. They are, for the most part, conscientious, well mannered, and respectful of other motorists. On a lighter note, the following story humorously depicts the exactness and diligence exercised by a number of conscientious drivers.

Sitting on the side of the highway waiting to catch speeding drivers, a state trooper eyes a car puttering along at 22-mph. He thinks, "This driver is just as dangerous as a speeder," and pulls over the driver.

Approaching the car, he notices that there are five elderly ladies, two in the front seat and three in the back, eyes wide and white as ghosts.

The driver, obviously confused, says to him, "Officer, I don't understand. I was doing exactly the speed limit! What seems to be the problem?"

"Ma'am," the officer replies, "you weren't speeding, but you should know that driving slower than the speed limit can also be a danger to other drivers."

"Slower than the speed limit?" she asked. "No sir, I was doing the speed limit exactly...22 miles an hour!" the old woman says a bit proudly.

The state trooper, trying to contain a chuckle, explains to her that "22" is the route number, not the speed limit. A bit embarrassed, the woman grinned and thanked the officer for pointing out her error." But before I let you go, Ma'am, I have to ask...Is everyone in this car OK? These women seem awfully shaken and they haven't muttered a single peep this whole time," the officer questioned.

"Oh, they'll be all right in a minute officer, we just got off of Route 75." [6]

Driving Persona

The conscientious style has an all-embracing need for order—on the road as well as in daily life. This style is based on fundamental traits of compulsivity, control, and self-consciousness. Beneath their compliancy is a dutiful respect for the law as well as for others on the road. Certain attributes of this style resemble the respectful style, as described by Theodore Millon,[7] portraying an individual with a highly organized behavioral appearance, a polite interpersonal conduct, and a restrained affective expression.

Rules provide the necessary structure required by this personality style, and since the law is of paramount importance, regulations are carried out, albeit at times, rigidly. For example, even if local traffic were very light and virtually non-existent on a particularly early hour of the morning, the conscientious individual, much to the chagrin of the hurried motorist behind him or her, wouldn't even consider turning right on red if not permitted. Not only would the action be illegal with the possibility of jeopardizing personal safety, but also, and more importantly, the conscientious personality would feel guilty and anxious about the infraction, since this action would be violating an internal code of conduct.

Systematic in their approach toward life, this style normally follows the same daily regimen with extreme regularity, rarely veering from the reliability that guarantees orderly control. Once they have established the best route from point *A* to point *B*, they master that route and rarely experiment with new ones. This style would typically choose a route for convenience, seldom selecting it for another reason, such as aesthetic advantage. Rarely, too, would anyone find their cars littered with old fast-food wrappers or soft drink cans on the floor. Have you ever been annoyed, if not irritated, by the dents and scratches left by inconsiderate motorists in a parking lot? If you think you "see red," place yourself in the shoes of the conscientious driver. These individuals may see various shades of red upon noticing the damage, though they would rarely voice their outrage. As an aside, one can easily avoid these annoyances by parking next a conscientious driver. To be sure, their vehicles are perfectly aligned, centered exactly between the lines, immaculately clean, and of course, "dent free." Conscientious individuals are meticulous about the care and maintenance of their vehicles, taking great pride in their appearance and performance. At times, though, they become self-absorbed, and cannot see the forest for the trees. In focusing on the details of life, they can easily overlook the bigger picture. The self-imposed internal pressure to "get something right" may in the end lead to their undoing. The maxim, *the hurrier they go, the behinder they get,* may fittingly apply to these drivers.

The Conscientious Pattern

Conscientious drivers seemingly muse, "If everyone did what they were supposed to do, it would be a wonderful world." That is, if all the motorists obeyed the rules of the road, traffic would proceed in a much less chaotic manner. In so doing, they can easily develop a tendency to feel ethically and morally superior to others. These individuals tend to be extremely cautious on the road, with the majority of drivers, as may be expected, preferring to use the middle lane, traveling at reasonable speeds with the flow of traffic for maximum safety and conformity. Nearly 70% drive within five miles per hour of the posted speed limit, with females appearing to drive slightly faster. "Rules are made to be strictly obeyed," could well be their highway mantra. Etiquette and courtesy are qualities that are also expected of other motorists on the road. The conscientious personality fully endorses and lives by the golden rule. These highly disciplined individuals, however, tend to lean toward perfectionism in all facets of their lives, which ultimately can become their downfall.

Of the total number of respondents, 12% comprise this personality pattern. Compared to the general population, conscientious drivers are more likely to buy a compact car, suggesting that the high mileage efficiency of smaller vehicles may reflect the conscientious personality's efficiency of operation, particularly with the rising cost of gasoline. Likely attributed to perfectionistic tendencies, merely 68% of these individuals consider themselves better drivers than other motorists, with younger motorists

23

expressing greater confidence in their driving ability than older motorists. Not surprisingly, more than 95% wear seatbelts, with the same percentage using directional indicators when switching lanes.

Vehicle Model Preferences for the Conscientious Pattern

Luxury	14%
Midsized	21%
Compact	37%
Light Truck	27%
Other	01%

Conscientious drivers consider vehicles to be a necessity of life—an economical means of conveyance, rather than mere expensive toys used for pleasurable excursions. In driving, as with most other regular activities, diligence, carefulness, and attention to detail are foremost concerns. Conscientious drivers prefer primary-colored vehicles, selecting earth tones as a second choice. Males lean toward primary colors, while females opt for softer earth tones.

Color Preferences for the Conscientious Pattern

White	19%
Earth Tones	30%
Primary Colors	33%
Black	17%
Other	01%

Rage on the Road

During moments of stress, the conscientious individuals hold tenaciously to the rules of the road, largely unyielding and determined in their compliance. With a strong ability to effectively control their impulses, merely 8% tend to remain angry following an irritable incident that is triggered by another motorist. Nonetheless, when angered and placed in untenable situations, these individuals can respond harshly and become overly critical. Although adherence to the rules of the road is an admirable quality, conscientious individuals, being over-controlled, can become unbending in observing them. An overly strict observance of the rules includes internal controls where a tight rein is also held on their expression of feelings and emotions.

A pressing need for control can also unearth an underlying compulsivity in the conscientious individual, and with concomitant rigidity, can easily lead to indecisive behaviors. The conscientious individual's indecisiveness, for example, can be most noticeable when merging onto an expressway. Driving behind these vehicles may present a trying time for the unfortunate driver who happens to be following when indecision strikes the conscientious driver. Certain variables that these individuals cannot control, namely, other vehicles, can readily cause indecision, if not consternation, on their part. When merging onto an expressway, for example, compulsively driven individuals may not necessarily have total confidence in their driving ability, not to mention their perception of the abilities of other motorists. They may instinctively speed up and then suddenly slow down, unsure of their ability to merge safely and cleanly. This indecisiveness often perplexes other motorists behind them.

In extreme conditions, a small fraction of these individuals may exhibit ritualistic behaviors. The rigidity that is common to these individuals can interfere with their ability to make even the simplest decisions. Though these individuals appear quite reserved and composed on the exterior, they can become easily conflicted internally. When aggressive impulses emerge, these individuals can become extremely anxious and lose control. Though they attempt to harness their urges, methods to regain control often prove unsuccessful.   Disrupted by intrusive thoughts and urges, they can develop excessive rituals, such as repeated hand washing or constantly returning to check things. When on the road, they may return to ensure that they had not struck a pedestrian or a stray animal if they were to hear a thump on the roadway. Subsequently, their normal controls become ineffective, and they are compelled to repeat the rituals. Varied compulsions inevitably harness obtrusive obsessions, reducing anxiety and distress, thereby controlling the unwanted aggressive urges. Anger most often is directed inwardly, with the repeated compulsions helping to maintain equilibrium.   The repetition of these rituals serves to bolster the individual's confidence while keeping the disturbing impulses at bay. This following edited story illustrates an extreme example of compulsivity.

The Conscientious Pattern

I got to my car park nice and early. I was about twenty minutes too early so I decided to sit quietly for a bit in the car and listen to the radio. A little red hatchback parked next to me, and I watched the ritual begin.

The driver got out, locked her driver's door, and went to the back passenger door on her side. She then unlocked it and opened it. Then she closed it, checked it and moved to the hatch. She unlocked that, opened it, closed it, and checked it again.

Following this, she proceeded to come around my side and do the same thing to both doors. All I heard was scratch, scratch, scratch. I got a teeny bit annoyed. I was thinking, "What on earth is going on," as I could see that all the doors were locked.

She hesitated.

She opened the door and locked it again. Instead of just leaving the godforsaken car, she actually went to the driver's door and opened it again. I was stunned.

The hatch was next. Unlock, open, lock, and check. Then she started the treacherous journey along the side of my car to the front door. "The door is locked. You locked it four times already," I said to myself.

She lumbered back to her driver's door quickly as her weight would allow and this time lent over and locked each door from the inside...unlocking them, then locking them. I finally had enough and needed to leave my car. As I was walking away, I then looked back at my car, satisfied in the knowledge it was locked once and for all, and began to walk to work. [8]

Stress-Free Driving Rx

Very few conscientious drivers are prone to remain angry following a provocation on the road. Angry outbursts are rare. They normally avoid confrontation on the road by simply blocking out annoyances. Though they are not confrontational, these individuals, however, are not immune to external stressors. Because of their need for order, a considerable degree of anxiety might be experienced when they perceive "things are not right." Though, to lessen moderately severe compulsivity found in some conscientious drivers who experience disabling stress on the road and find it unmanageable, the following prescriptions may provide relief.

- ✓ Reduce overwhelming anxiety through various coping techniques, such as visualizing a serene scene. For example, envision a tranquil winding road along the seashore, while you wind your way through congested traffic.

- ✓ Lessen negative thinking, primarily attribution of blame. When another motorist blatantly ignores the rules, simply "let it go." Say to yourself, "Just concentrate on your own driving."

- ✓ If you are troubled by ritualistic behaviors, such as returning to your car to insure that it is locked, interrupt the cycle by challenging your distorted thinking. Simply tell your inner self to "stop."

- ✓ Develop a balance in your life between self-mandatory (things you have to do) and non-mandatory (things you enjoy doing) activities.

✓ Choose a longer, scenic route to work one day for a change of pace, focusing on the beauty of the newly discovered road.

✓ Let go of the need to create a "perfect" world. For example, the next time you hand-wash your car, simply let it air dry, leaving a few spots on the hood. It will be fine. The car will still operate efficiently.

In Summary

In this chapter, we have examined the conscientious pattern of driving, a style that is cautious, conscientious, and law-abiding. As with every facet of their lives, details are carefully considered and planned. This driver has an absolute respect for the rules and obeys them to the letter. This category of personality, more so than others, personifies the *safe* drivers on the road. Nevertheless, when confronted with uncertainty on the road, the conscientious driver may become conflicted and lean toward indecisiveness. In the extreme, this driver can exercise excessive compulsive and ritualistic behaviors, causing a fair degree of anxiety to self and other.

Next, we consider the conscientious driver's polar opposite, namely, the impulsive driver or uncontrolled dimension of personality. As is evident, one pattern embraces the influence of control, while its opposite lacks this influence. The conscientious driver characterizes the unemotional driver, one who internalizes angry emotion, thereby minimizing the tendency for aggressiveness on the road. The impulsive driver, on the other hand, directly expresses emotion. There exists a marked contrast between these two personality styles, namely, control versus *dys*-control, of one's anger expression. The following chapter further examines the impulsive pattern.

Self Tune-up

When you occasionally have an urge to "veer off" your course, slowly bring your attention back to the matter at hand—namely, driving toward your goal. Refocus your attention and feel the energy in your hands gripping the steering wheel. Squeeze the wheel tightly, and loudly shout, "I am in control. I don't want to submit to these sudden whims." Press your grip tightly until the distracting urges lessen. Then ease up slightly. Repeat the exercise if urges resurface.

---

❸ The Impulsive Pattern

Unlike the reserved demeanor of the conscientious driver, its polar opposite ordinarily displays imprudent, hasty, and rash behaviors, depicting the style of the impulsive driver. If you find yourself, at times, "spinning out of control," the following identifying characteristics may describe your driving style.

- Acts on sudden urges, such as speeding "just for the thrill of it"

- Feels that turn signal indicators are not always necessary

- Engages in daring behaviors

- Urges are uncontrollable

- Has an excessive number of moving traffic violations

- Feels slighted when cut off on the road

- Seemingly always rushing to get somewhere

- Servicing the car not a priority

- Fleeting enthusiasm for projects

- Has difficulty managing anger

- Rarely considers the consequences of actions

While many individuals often have an urge to "do something" spontaneously or uncharacteristically act out, this type of behavior is second nature for the impulsive pattern who exhibits little control over surging impulses. Impulsive individuals are spontaneous, carefree, and often impervious to risk. They are openly curious and inquisitive about life's purpose, always exploring stimulus-seeking behaviors. Though they are highly enthusiastic about the pursuits in which they engage, their attention span tends to be transitory. As a result, their initial enthusiasm becomes short-lived.

They often act on a "whim," giving little or no thought to the consequences of their actions. Danger rarely seems a concern, a trait often evidenced in young and overconfident drivers. They habitually engage in daring behaviors primarily because it feels good. Such "feel good" behavior is the vehicle used to achieve immediate gratification in their lives. Unexpected and spontaneous decisions govern the activities of these drivers, as one can immediately observe the unpredictable characteristics displayed. A passenger, for example, may ask the driver, "Why did you do that?" as he or she veers off the road for no apparent reason. The impulsive drivers merely don a sheepish grin, unsure of their motivation for the spontaneous maneuver.

Urges, unquestionably, are uncontrollable for the impulsive driver. During a conversation about road rage, a friend related an atypical incident that he had experienced.

32

Matt normally is a mild-mannered, quiet and reserved law-abiding motorist. While he was driving along a four-lane expressway on a particularly hot and humid day, he said he just got "the urge" to tailgate another motorist because the driver was going too slowly. When questioned about the imprudence of his actions, he simply stated, "I don't know why I did it. I just felt like doing it." He "gave in" to his impulse, typifying this style of driving. He had awakened his "hidden Hyde." Spontaneous urges are quite natural occurrences for this driver, acting on many of them. Regrettably, observance of the rules of the road takes a "back seat" to one's impulsive urges. Emotionally driven, this individual reacts purely on whims, unmindful of the consequences. In general, a "devil-may-care" attitude could aptly describe this personality pattern.

Driving Persona

These individuals are impetuous on the road, having a vigorous, adventurous, and noticeably uncontrolled driving style. The impulsive drivers are daring in their pursuits, with risky behaviors being the norm. These drivers usually "wear their feelings on their sleeves" and thrust themselves full throttle into every activity or interest they undertake.

Exploring new vistas seems second nature to this pattern, as their thoughts quickly race from one stimulus to another. It would not be uncommon for the impulsive driver to suddenly swerve off Interstate 90 and onto the exit ramp after eyeing a sign, for instance, advertising Niagara Falls.

Perhaps fantasizing about a roll down the Falls, they seek yet another stimulating adventure. These individuals enjoy their freedom, as well as the risks these freedoms entail. As with spontaneously changing one's direction to visit the Falls, impulsive individuals do not need any particular reason to "shift gears" other than to say, "I'd like to do it." Suffice it to say, much of the time their moods are variable, and behaviors erratic.

On the road, impulsive individuals usually "feel the world" through their emotions rather than evaluating a situation rationally. Other drivers perceive them as driving too fast, or, depending on their mood, too slowly. The impulsive driver then acts accordingly—or rather, whimsically, as noted in the following experience.

> I recall one day traveling along a rather barren stretch of Interstate 94 on the Lower Peninsula of Michigan, when a group of individuals in another automobile zoomed past my vehicle at an unusually high rate of speed. One mile along the expressway, I found myself passing the same vehicle that was now barely maintaining the speed as the group was fully absorbed in conversation.

A routine and monotonous drive along a dull expressway makes these individuals noticeably restless, bored, and impetuous. These individuals apparently realize their risky, impulsive behaviors on the road, since merely 60% acknowledge that they are more cautious than other motorists, yet 75% of this pattern state that they are better drivers than the average driver.

Impulsive individuals frequently find themselves in a hurry, oftentimes rushing through traffic, though not necessarily because they are pressed for time. It is simply their nature. They naturally act without worrying about the consequences or the motivation for their impulsive actions. Most road behaviors, such as cutting across several lanes of traffic or suddenly exiting a ramp, occur without deliberation and with minimal consideration of others. "Impulsive individuals' thinking comes 'off the top of the head,' with their actions being speedy, abrupt, and unplanned." [9]

This pattern comprised approximately 8% of the survey respondents. This total likely reflects the number of impulsive individuals found in the driving public. Males, by a margin of nearly three to one, make up this pattern.

Vehicle Model Preferences for the Impulsive Pattern

Luxury Sedan	13%
Midsized	27%
Compact	22%
Light Truck	36%
Other	02%

The preferred model of vehicle for both genders is the light truck, perhaps because of its daring appeal. On the road, you have likely observed these individuals. They have a penchant for determinedly merging into the faster lane of traffic. Seemingly forceful, these impulsive drivers may outwardly resemble the aggressive pattern. Both males and females having this pattern drive in the lane most convenient for them. Merely 70% wear seatbelts, the lowest percentage among all personality styles. Usually in a hurry, only 50% of this group states that they maintain a reasonable speed.

Not surprisingly, the primary-colored vehicles are clearly the colors of choice. Other than the vehicle color, it may prove difficult distinguishing these drivers from the aggressive driving pattern discussed later.

Color Preferences for the Impulsive Pattern

White	14%
Earth Tones	22%
Primary Colors	38%
Black	22%
Other	04%

Rage on the Road

Literally in an instant, the impulsive style can shift emotional gears. Inappropriate, intense emotion can be summoned with minimal provocation. Spontaneous mood swings can result in excessive displays of temper and unpredictable behavior. The "act on a whim" nature of these individuals combined with a rapid response makes for unpredictability as well as confusion for other drivers. As these motorists generally do not signal their intentions, one wonders whether they are careless or just forgetful. When traffic grinds to a halt, as it usually does in major cities during rush hours, other drivers simply shake their heads as the impulsive drivers choose to weave through traffic, "going nowhere quickly."

In our driving experiences, we have all come across this type of motorist. When an irate individual pulls up beside us, directly expressing angry emotion regarding something we had supposedly done, we are left merely scratching our heads and asking, "What did I do?" Impulsive behavior is not an unexpected occurrence on the road, with disruptive flare-ups more often the norm. As previously mentioned, impulsive behaviors can be erratic, from continually changing the channel on the radio to unpredictably racing closely to a slower vehicle's bumper. An example of such impetuous angry behavior that could not be constrained or controlled is presented in the following vignette.

> Jack liked to show-off and oftentimes chose to impress others with his driving. Tom, a coworker, needed a lift home from work one day and Jack offered him a ride, as it was on his way. Tom accepted gratefully.
>
> Jack's vehicle screeched, as his car peeled out of the company parking lot. "Smell the rubber?" Jack asked, as he shot a mischievous glance to Tom. Tom was speechless and, at that point, already wished he was anywhere but in a car with Jack.
>
> As Jack continued to accelerate down the road, he would weave in and out of traffic haphazardly until he came to a red light. After the light changed to

green, the car in front of him resumed driving at the posted speed.

This was unacceptable to Jack, and so he began creeping closer and closer to the Chevy, while sounding his horn. By this time, the driver of the other car was aware of Jack's impatience, but rather than speed up a bit to appease him, the other driver decided to drive below the speed limit.

That was it! Jack was infuriated and continued to tailgate. Suddenly, the other motorist stopped abruptly and—you guessed it—Jack rear-ended him. Jack was stunned, shook his head and asked, "What just happened here?"

Tom and Jack got out of the car to assess any damage. Just before approaching the other driver, Tom nudged Jack and remarked, "Perhaps this may answer your question," as he pointed to the bumper sticker that read,

"If you can read this, I can slam on my brakes and SUE YOU!"

One may ask why do such drivers risk endangering the lives of other motorists? Is even an ounce of judgment exercised? What causes people, literally and figuratively, to lose control on the highways? People wouldn't think of cutting in line at a supermarket, yet cutting in front of another on the road seems to be acceptable behavior, perhaps attributed to anonymity. Confounding such an individual's emotional state, however, may be an untreated condition, such as ADHD, Mania, or Intermittent Explosive Disorder (discussed below under the Aggressive Pattern). For a certain percentage, habitually erratic driving, such as tailgating a slower vehicle, may indeed find its genesis in an underlying condition. For most, though, it is simply a style. Unlike the controlled individual, who is accustomed to meticulous planning, the impulsive driver, for the most part, lacks proper judgment. This individual remains unmindful of the consequences the controlled driver would necessarily consider before taking action. In short, because the impulsive drivers lack proper judgment, they spontaneously act on their impulses, rather than rationally thinking through their actions. They require minimal provocation to express their anger and react aggressively to the most innocuous circumstances with unleashed rage, oftentimes, to the dismay and utter surprise of the victimized motorist. "Aggressive variants of the impulsive style cause the individual to act on forceful whims, with their aims being quick, concrete gains. Irritable moods, though transitory, can ignite very forceful behavioral outbursts, being noticeably compounded by their whimsical and unpredictable nature." [10]   Thus, impulsive responses can be swift, unpredictable, and intense. For the majority of these drivers, however, reactive anger is short-lived. The defining quality of these individuals is the immediacy of their actions, with concomitant lack of judgment.

Stress-Free Driving Rx

Impulsive behavior is an expected occurrence on the roads, with disruptive flare-ups being more the norm than the exception.   The lack of focus, particularly at critical moments on the road, coupled with *dys*-controlled erratic behaviors can easily lead to unnecessary fender-benders or more serious incidents. Impulsive aggressive behavior is likely occurring with greater frequency than may be realized by these individuals. Impulsive drivers express their anger quickly and directly. Although anger is transitory in the majority of impulsive drivers, nearly 20% of this group is normally prone to remain angry following a provocation on the road. The actions usually taken by these individuals can be likened to a car with no brakes, that is, once rolling along in gear, this individual is difficult to stop. The following prescriptions may provide relief for individuals within this group.

- ✓ A safe and structured approach to driving, such as concentrating on maintaining the posted speed limits, using turn signal indicators, etc., can serve as the cornerstone in reducing impulsive actions on the road.

- ✓ Reduce the number of emotional urges by pausing a moment to consider the rationale of your actions in relation to the other motorist's intent. Essentially, think about what you're about to do, rather than reacting.

- ✓ Gradually reframe ways of defining the environment by designing adaptive and positive strategies, such as pulling off to the side of the road when angry impulses begin to surface.

- ✓ Curb inconsistent and aggressive attitudes by considering alternate courses of action. For example, after persistently weaving through traffic, ask yourself, "How much time did that actually save me?"

✓ If continued impulsivity results in increased numbers of moving violations or traffic accidents, perhaps behavioral therapy may prove beneficial.

✓ Control of emotions and behaviors can be learned and rehearsed through stress-reduction techniques, such as deep-breathing exercises, when identified impulsive urges tend to surface.

In Summary

In this chapter we examined the characteristics of the impulsive driver. While the conscientious individual is controlled in most behaviors, and rigidly orders the environment, the impulsive personality does not function with any binding internal strictures. They can "let loose" at any time, even when minimally provoked. Impulsive individuals impetuously act and react on the road, without considering the consequences of their actions. Their rash behaviors merely serve to perplex other drivers.

Impulsive drivers are adventurous and daring, having variants of aggressiveness. On the road, as in life, they act on whims. Their behaviors are often unexpected and as such, produce a degree of angst for other motorists. A "devil-may-care" attitude is typical of this pattern. Carefree and spontaneous, impulsive drivers rarely evaluate a situation fully. Inappropriate emotion normally drives this pattern on and off the road. Minimal provocation from another motorist can easily lead to aggressive reactions.

Unlike the impulsive personality, who takes chances and jeopardizes the lives of other drivers, we now turn to the courteous pattern, whose style of behavior is characterized by politeness, accommodation, and safe driving.

Self Tune-up

Counter disturbing, impetuous thoughts with rational thinking; curb any intrusive thoughts by substituting balanced rational thoughts for random spontaneous thoughts to help you arrive at sound decisions on the road.

If the ambiguity causes distress, take a moment, and calm yourself. Pull off to the side of the rode for a rest break. Breathe slowly through your abdomen. Then begin to exercise your neck muscles by tilting your head toward the right for a count of ten, with each second tilting your head lower until you touch your shoulder. Imagine that you are emptying your mind of the distressing thoughts. Then shift to your left side, similarly tilting your head for another ten seconds in the opposite direction. When calmness returns, be on your way!

---

❹ The Courteous Pattern

Ralph Waldo Emerson once said, "Life is not so short but that there is always time enough for courtesy. " With regard to driving behavior, one never needs to be so inconsiderate as to deprive another of thoughtfulness and tolerance. It isn't difficult to recognize this good-natured personality on the road. The following characteristics suggest a courteous personality pattern.

- Promotes safe and cautious driving habits

- Allows others to assume responsibility and make decisions

- Normally docile and unassuming on the road

- Unsure of self-abilities, with respect to general driving skills

- Desires the company of others and does not care to drive alone

- Observes all traffic laws

- Exercises patience with other motorists on the road

- Generally feels anxious when driving in congested traffic

- Prefers to let someone else drive

- Respects the rights of other motorists and pedestrians

More than other patterns, the courteous driver is cooperative, obliging, and accommodating on the road. The individual with whom we will become acquainted in this chapter demonstrates the characteristics found in more chivalrous societies. Characteristically unassuming, these individuals respectfully defer to other motorists. Quite simply, they are polite and maintain a genuine concern for other drivers. Normally adept at defensive driving, they take preventive means to safeguard themselves as well as others from hazardous and risky situations. Underlying these qualities is a willingness to acquiesce to the wishes of others. For instance, the courteous driver will contentedly allow another vehicle to merge into the flow of bumper-to-bumper expressway traffic and even slow down to provide smoother access for the merging motorist. Courteous behavior is not necessarily practiced for safety reasons, but more so out of respect for the other motorist.

These drivers are overly accommodating in adapting their road behaviors to fit another's needs, rarely engaging in forceful behaviors. Along with the timid driver, this pattern is perhaps among the least likely of the eight personality styles to express aggression when driving. Similar in some respects to the timid driver, the courteous style tends to be docile in demeanor, looking to others to make decisions on the road as well as in life. During an unexpected road closure, for example, one may observe this driver craning his or her neck checking to see the direction others are taking. These drivers often could be categorized as "followers" in life as on the highway, allowing others to take the lead. They are content to remain behind the scenes, letting others occupy center stage. On the road, they simply blend in rather unobtrusively with the flow of traffic.

Courteous individuals are perceived as being sober in all endeavors and genuine in their pursuits. Generous and openhanded, this personality pattern easily becomes attached to people. They completely trust others, oftentimes unequivocally and without reservation, giving them the benefit of the doubt. While not unduly timorous as the timid style of personality, the courteous style tends to be extremely cautious, if not somewhat apprehensive on the road. Given a choice, though, between being behind the wheel and sitting in the passenger seat, they would prefer someone else do the driving. These individuals are real "classics" when behind the wheel, resembling a throwback in some ways to the days when driving was enjoyable, and most motorists demonstrated civility and regard for the rights of other drivers.

Driving Persona

The courteous pattern comprised 23% of the drivers surveyed—the largest among the eight personality groups measured. The courteous style is characterized by a steady, safe, and consistent driving manner. Courteous drivers are also sociable, obedient, and friendly on the road. This motorist readily adjusts and adapts to the behaviors of other drivers, as well as to road conditions. To some degree, we can say that these individuals "drive with others in mind."

Courteous drivers obey the rules of the road not necessarily out of a fear of "being cited," but more so out of deference to others and the law. Responsive to the needs of others on the road, they try to oblige another driver whenever possible. For example, at a four-way stop when drivers reach their respective stop signs at roughly the same time, the courteous individual will allow the other motorists to proceed by displaying a friendly wave of the hand or simply waiting for them to proceed. Some personality patterns may insist that since they are positioned to the right of the other motorist, they have the legal right of way when vehicles simultaneously reach a four-way stop—and will "enforce" their right-of-way. The courteous driver, however, politely allows the other driver the right-of-way, regardless of determining who is right or wrong in the eyes of the law. A list of courteous driving behaviors, to include obeying posted speed limits, concentrating on driving without the distraction of mobile phones, and maintaining a safe distance developed by the Coalition for Consumer Health and Safety (CCHS) [11] are behaviors normally practiced by the courteous driver.

Expectedly, these individuals tend to be cautious on the road (81% feel that they are more cautious than other motorists) and prefer to drive in the right lane with the flow of traffic for maximum safety and conformity. Nearly 30% of both genders representing this pattern usually drive within five miles over the posted speed limit, with females likely exceeding these limits slightly more often than their male counterparts.

While safe and cautious, some drivers in this group, however, are openly aware of their reticence with respect to driving skills. Merely 63% of the females and 70% of the males consider themselves to be better drivers than others. Younger drivers, though, appear to be more confident about their driving ability when compared to older age groups. The majority of courteous motorists prefer to drive American-made cars, the only such group having this preference. Women tend to gravitate toward compact vehicles, while men are more inclined to choose the midsize model. Drivers in the 40 to 50-year-old range account for the majority of light trucks purchased by this personality pattern. Rather conservative in their approach, they likely opt for safety, dependability, and reliability, rather than flare in choice of automobiles.

Vehicle Model Preferences for the Courteous Pattern

Luxury Sedan	09%
Midsized	32%
Compact	30%
Light Truck	28%
Other	01%

With respect to vehicle color, primary-colored vehicles and earth tones are equally preferred choices by courteous drivers. Females tend to lean toward primary colors, while males opt for earth tones. The exception to these preferences is the middle-aged bracket of drivers who opt for black-colored vehicles.

Color Preferences for the Courteous Pattern	
White	13%
Earth Tones	33%
Primary Colors	34%
Black	19%
Other	01%

Rage on the Road

Normally docile in nature, courteous drivers naturally shun conflict and make every effort to avoid confrontation. Yet, precisely because of their social acquiescence on the road, courteous drivers occasionally "ruffle the feathers" of the hurried motorist. Take, for example, the growing number of drivers who appear to be "color-challenged" when approaching the traffic signal. They seem to think that the cautionary yellow is a signal indicating that one should accelerate in order to advance hurriedly through the intersection before the signal turns red and the camera snaps. The cautiousness and at times apprehension displayed by the courteous driver can then be a source of dismay to many of the more assertive motorists. This is particularly evident when following too closely behind these individuals, as they vigilantly prepare to stop yards before the amber signal turns to red, whether or not a camera is positioned at the intersection. Such situations can indeed provoke a potentially explosive, if not jarring situation.

As previously mentioned, courteous personalities, along with the timid driving pattern, are arguably the least likely of all personality styles to express outward aggression on the road. True to their appeasing and conciliatory nature, clearly 96% of these drivers claim that they do not remain angry following an annoyance on the road, the highest percentage among all patterns surveyed. Unlike the more hostile personality patterns, the courteous individuals tend to suppress negative emotion, rarely expressing their displeasure outwardly. Though, as the following story illustrates, this pattern can indeed reach a "breaking point" and on occasion, exhibit passive-aggressive tendencies.

> It was a slippery and snowy December 26th a few years ago and Greg decided to join the after-Christmas shoppers to exchange a couple of gifts. He didn't mind the crowds. Upon exiting the mall, he noticed a woman desperately circling the lot in search of a coveted parking place, but to no avail. Being the nice person that he is, he approached her car and motioned for her to roll down the window. Then he told her to back up and take his spot.

> The woman smiled at Greg, but was obviously too engrossed in her phone call. She gave a quick wave of gratitude with her cell phone in hand and proceeded to back up her vehicle while still talking. In her attempt to drive in reverse, she zigzagged to where Greg was standing and nearly bumped into him. Shaken by her near miss, he got out of his car once again—and maybe in a too authoritative

tone—told the driver that she should put away the cell phone and concentrate on her driving.

Her mood quickly changed as she screamed uncontrollably, telling him it was none of his business what she did. Fearing an unnecessary confrontation, Greg more quickly began to vacate the parking space. At that point, however, he was so shaken that his bumper nudged hers as he exited, but continued on without stopping. She became livid and quickly dialed up the police to report Greg's license and the "hit and run" incident.

When the officer caught up with poor Greg, he said nothing in his defense, as he was dumbfounded by the turn of events. He just sat there frozen in more ways than one. The officer said that Greg appeared to be a victim of another person's rage, but that he should have stopped at the scene of the mishap. Greg acknowledged that he shouldn't have permitted the other driver's anger to paralyze his good judgment and could only remark, "So much for a good deed."

As demonstrated through Greg's encounter, and in keeping with their psychological makeup, the courteous pattern is accommodating by nature, though may be compelled to express varying behaviors, at times being overly passive-aggressive. When confronted, this cooperative and tolerant style can become transformed into an anxious distraught individual such as Greg and express their displeasure through "flighty" behaviors by simply "driving away" to avoid an altercation. Rarely, though, do courteous drivers intentionally annoy other motorists and, as a matter of course, customarily go out of their way to avoid confrontation whenever and wherever possible. There exists within this pattern a strong desire to please. Being overly accommodating, personal driving attitudes are usually adapted to fit another's needs, causing minimal consternation for other motorists.

Stress-Free Driving Rx

The courteous driver arguably is the least likely of all patterns to become irritated or express anger directly. Less than 5% of these motorists experience prolonged irritation on the road. Nonetheless, this style, on occasion, does become anxious and apprehensive, particularly when confronted. At such times, they may be prone to act out, albeit in a "flighty" fashion. To ameliorate troubling anxiety, the following prescriptions may prove useful.

- ✓ Identify anxiety-producing stimuli (e.g., racing heartbeat, moist palms) and face them squarely through self-reassurance. Remind yourself that you are a safe and cautious driver and that these positive qualities will prevail when negative and anxious situations arise.

- ✓ Practice relaxation skills on and off the road. While driving on a congested highway, for example, inhale deeply and hold the breath for a moment, then slowly exhale, as you count down from 10.

- ✓ Direct angry emotions appropriately, targeting the sources of frustration, instead of suppressing negative feelings.

- ✓ When you become angry, hurt, or disappointed by the behaviors of others, make an effort to be non-accusatory, though exercise your assertive rights.

   ✓   Reduce stress by strengthening assertiveness skills. For example, practice being firm and resolute in your decisions.

In Summary

This chapter examined the characteristics of the courteous driver. Considerate and safety-conscious on the road, they do not take chances, nor do they place themselves or other drivers in jeopardy. Courteous behavior is practiced out of respect for other motorists. In characterizing the style of the courteous pattern, we can say that these individuals are essentially non-assertive, ingratiating, and accommodating. This pattern is expectedly among the most polite and civil motorists on the road. Ordinarily, along with the timid style, they are seemingly the least likely personality style to demonstrate rage on the road. Normally docile in nature, courteous drivers naturally shun conflict and make every effort to avoid confrontation. When confronted, however, this cooperative style can become transformed into an anxious distraught individual, usually expressing their displeasure through withdrawal behaviors. The courteous style is non-confrontational and typically acquiesces to the wishes or demands of others. They employ safe driving habits and avoid confrontation at all costs.

While the courteous style practices safe driving and may be considered the most trusting of personality styles, the distrusting or guarded driver is quite the opposite. The cynical style measures safe driving in terms of defensiveness on the road, though unlike the courteous driver, is   readily provoked into aggressive behavior following an irritable encounter with another motorist. The cynical diver will be discussed further in the next chapter.

Self Tune-up

When you find yourself tensing up, feeling an unusual nervous tightness in your muscles, go to the muscle group in which you first felt the tightness. Continue concentrating on your driving, and tighten that muscle group.

For instance, if your head feels tight, scrunch your forehead as tightly as possible, and hold the tension for about 10 seconds. Then slowly relax the tension in your forehead as you down-count to zero. After releasing the tension, think about the sense of calmness it brings. Repeat the exercise again in other muscle groups, keeping at least one hand firmly on the wheel.

❺ The Cynical Pattern

Beyond the protective shielding that envelops the courteous pattern, the cynical style, ever vigilant and cautious, measures safe driving in terms of one's defensive-driving in relation to other motorists. Their makeup reveals a skilled and competent, yet warily defensive driver, vigilantly monitoring another's behaviors on the road. Consider these identifying characteristics applicable to the cynical driver.

- Exercises unfailing vigilance on the road

- Easily becomes irritated with erratic motorists

- Questions driving skills of other motorists

- Clearly understands the nuances of driving

- Becomes sullen and resentful when stopped for a moving violation

- Bears quiet grudges against other motorists

- Takes pride in personal driving ability

- Often rationalizes and projects blame onto others

- Can be intolerant of other motorists

- Mood and disposition often contingent on situational events

- Quick to blame others

With respect to individual motorists, the structural form of this pattern ranges from normal vigilance to neurotic suspiciousness, from healthy skepticism to unyielding cynicism. Inherently distrustful, these drivers stubbornly guard their personal space and are overtly hypersensitive toward others' perceived "indiscretions." This style is always mindful of the other driver's movements. For instance, another motorist's merging too closely between vehicles into the flow of traffic may be perceived as an invasion of space and cause for concern. Keenly aware of the nuances of the road, these individuals alertly defend their territorial space when driving. Unlike the prototypical aggressive driver for whom another's space is anything but sacred and who will seize it without consideration of the other driver's rights, cynical individuals will not intentionally usurp another's space. They will, however, vigorously defend their own space. The normal response or reaction when one invades the space of this driver likely is disdain, if not contempt for the "violator's" behavior. They might cynically shrug it off as simply another breach of road etiquette and mutter a few choice words, or if the situation warrants, discharge a sudden fury. Being skeptical on the road in order to avert intruders, cynical drivers closely protect their boundaries, ever ready to take "necessary" action. More so with this personality pattern than others, cynical drivers let down their "psychic guard" as they begin to age and mature. Possibly, a matter of slowing reflexes comes into play or simply a question of maturity, as they pay less attention to other motorists and concentrate more closely on their own driving behaviors. Like a good wine, these individuals seemingly mellow with age, becoming less inclined to mobilize their aggression in defense of their territorial space. With the passing years, as suggested, these personalities may likely "mellow" and exercise more tolerance, becoming less sensitive to the "antics" of other motorists, and the vagaries of life in general. With this in mind, let us now look deeper into the driving style of the cynical personality.

Driving Persona

Cynical individuals practice defensive driving and pride themselves in their ability to maneuver around the intrusions of other motorists. As this style of defensive driving is synonymous with vigilance or guardedness, the standards of safe and cautious driving are always paramount in this individual's road behavior. Regarding one's alertness, though, the term cynical also connotes a hypersensitivity that turns attention away from self and directs it toward the other motorist, particularly with respect to any perceived slights on the road. For example, when "errors in judgment" are perceived as personal infractions on the road, these individuals are quick to assess blame and outwardly point the finger of accusation.

Similar to the conscientious drivers, cynical drivers fully know the rules of road and normally observe them, expecting others to do the same. Though the cynical style is quite astute when appraising the attributes of others, their sensitive antennae sometimes tend to collect too much data. They readily measure and evaluate not only the actions, but also the intent of other drivers. This practice, however, can also be a double-edged sword. While they may quickly gauge the other's intentions, their judgments of the motives may not necessarily be accurate. Consequently, their perceptions of another's motives may be skewed, often reacting with a sense of urgent confrontation, rather than rationally analyzing the objectivity of the situation. It may not be unusual for this pattern to play "the enforcer" by tapping the brakes, signaling that another motorist is too close. Also, rather than changing to a slower lane, they might simply slow down when another is perceived to be tailgating. In scanning, or more precisely, assessing the traffic around them, they are extremely sensitive to the temperaments of other drivers. Yet again, accurateness may come into question, as they tend to assume without fully verifying the nature and intent of another's actions. Another's bumper sticker, for example, with very small lettering that cautions, "If you can read this, you are too close" provides cynical drivers a very useful insight, so to speak, into the mind of the message bearer, whom they judge accordingly. They remain constantly on guard, always prepared for any real or imagined threat. The vast majority of this pattern, however, advocates safe driving practices, ever cautious in maintaining proper distance and reasonable speed limits.

Both men and women exhibiting this pattern prefer to drive with the flow of traffic; however, females tend to drive a little faster than their male counterparts. The majority of cynical drivers regularly prefer to use the right lane while on an expressway. One may assume that the right lane offers these drivers a clear, unobstructed view of the traffic lanes, a better perspective from which to observe the patterns of traffic. More than 90% of both genders regularly wear their seatbelts, and four out of five make known their intentions by using turn signals. It is interesting to note that although this style is overly vigilant on the road, merely 50% of these individuals rate themselves as better drivers than other motorists—the smallest percentage among all personality patterns.

The cynical pattern comprised slightly more than 8% of the survey respondents and likely reflects the percentage of "guarded" individuals in the driving public. With regard to vehicle preference, the compact vehicle narrowly edged out the light truck among this group. Female motorists prefer the compact cars, while the greater number of males leans toward light trucks.

Vehicle Model Preferences for the Cynical Pattern

Luxury Sedan	07%
Midsized	17%
Compact	39%
Light Truck	34%
Other	03%

With regard to vehicle color, black is the slight preference. Males tend to lean toward black-colored vehicles, while more females prefer primary-colored vehicles.

Color Preferences for the Cynical Pattern

White	17%
Earth Tones	21%
Primary Colors	28%
Black	29%
Other	05%

Rage on the Road

Normally cautious and careful when operating a vehicle, the habitual demeanor of the cynical driver can easily give way to negative emotion. These individuals are usually fearful that others will exploit them. Ever vigilant of the anticipated "ominous cloud on the horizon," their *personas* quickly can transform into faces filled with mistrust. On the road, as was previously mentioned, the cynical driver critically scans the environment for hidden meanings underlying the actions of others. Ever alert, these individuals are keenly perceptive. Nonetheless, during times of duress their judgments can become clouded, and subsequently, decisions are shaded with intolerance. Therefore, they tend to react swiftly and forcefully, with seemingly little provocation. Pulling into an open parking place ahead of them, for example, may be perceived as a direct affront, and could easily lead to a fiery confrontation. They can be quick to criticize another's driving behavior and just as quick to react in kind. In response to a perceived affront by another motorist, aggressive impulses can indeed be acted upon, particularly if the intentions of the other driver are interpreted as a threat.

Surrounding this style there is a nonspecific air of resentment toward others. Very few deeds escape their scrutiny. Certain variants of this pattern seem to be angry at the world—with no specific target toward which to direct their anger. Consider the following personal story of an incident that occurred on my way to work one morning. The actions of the angered individual expressed a rage that was direct and intentional. What prompted this driver's inappropriate display of anger? Apparently, "perceived contempt," or perhaps a driver who is habitually angry had seemingly found a convenient "target." Unfortunately, I was the unsuspecting target that morning.

> At 7:30 AM on a weekday morning, I was traveling my normal route through the downtown morning rush hour. As I cleared the Loop traffic, I was driving west along Chicago Avenue, a four-lane street. Approaching Wells, I stopped for the light in the outside lane from which I was going to make a left turn. Moments later, a female driver in a late model SUV pulled alongside me, stopping at the traffic signal in the right lane.

> While we were stopped at the red light, a city maintenance truck, seemingly out of nowhere, swerved into the intersection and stopped directly adjacent to the sewer cover, which incidentally was

directly positioned in front of the female driver's vehicle. It struck me as comical, and as I am known to do, I looked toward her and chuckled. That was surely a mistake I would learn several minutes later.

As the light turned green, I eased into the intersection, waiting for the oncoming traffic before I proceeded to turn left. As I crept into the intersection, the young woman slipped behind me and proceeded to thump my rear bumper. I looked into my rear view mirror and noticed that she was flustered.

It was just a mere tap, so I dismissed it as accidental and let it go. Then I inched a bit more into the intersection, at which time she again struck my bumper. I put my vehicle in neutral, pulled the emergency brake, and left it in the middle of the intersection. I got out of my Toyota to check the rear of my car for any damage and then walked back to her to ask what might be the problem.

As I approached her half-opened window, the young woman's face was a picture of fright as she explained, "I had nowhere to go because of the truck." I would have accepted, at minimum, an apology, however, she provided no apology and accepted no responsibility for her actions. I simply asked her what was her problem and advised her to make an appointment for an anger management class, then returned to my car still parked in the middle of the intersection. I made my left turn and continued on my way, trying to dismiss yet another driving frustration from my mind.

If such drivers believe that they might have been slighted, individuals demonstrating this style may directly "go after" other drivers (as evidenced in the above account). When they perceive to be wronged on the road, they act out. They harbor negative feelings after a provocative incident and may project delayed fury onto another unsuspecting motorist. Nearly 25% of this group remains upset following a disturbing incident, suggesting a proneness to sustained negative expression of anger. Aggression is manifested directly or indirectly, depending on the style's variant. Most express anger in a subtle, indirect way. Some, however, may express their aggression directly, often with a readiness to inflict harm on others. When driving alongside these individuals, they appear amenable and agreeable, that is, until others try to impose unexpected control over them. Signs of resentment and anger tend to surface as they resist doing what others expect of them. Their cautious, guarded demeanor can suddenly turn brazen, cold, and indifferent when provoked. When another motorist seemingly invades another's territorial space, moods can turn unpredictable, as evidenced in the following edited story from Sandy's advice column.

Dear Sandy,

I got my driver's license a little less than a year ago. I'm a good driver, cautious, etc. I've never been in an accident and I'm very attentive of other drivers' next moves. The problem is that when a driver pulls out on me or does something else like that, I get very angry. Sometimes I'll go faster and tailgate for a block or two or give bad looks. What's wrong with me? I'm normally a very calm person and a great driver. It's definitely not like me to have these reactions and I don't like them at all. How can I curb them? Whenever someone pulls out, I try to ignore it or think about something else. It just doesn't help. Thanks!   Mad Driver

Dear Mad Driver,

For some unknown reason, when certain people get behind the wheel, they seemingly lose their minds. What you have to keep in mind, of course, is your safety and just ignore them. Getting upset takes away from your feeling good, so you just have to realize that there is nothing you can do about it. Hopefully, you will set an example by driving correctly and politely. Just think of people who drive badly as people who have no respect for themselves or others. Try not to let it get to you, because you are only going to hurt yourself in the end, e.g., bad mood, retaliation, to name a few. Take a few deep breaths and just keep driving! Sandy [12]

Stress-Free Driving Rx

Cynical drivers can be counted among the safer drivers on the road. However, as mentioned earlier, if such drivers perceive an affront, the forceful variant found in some of these individuals will directly confront other drivers. This variant is more likely to respond to provocation than other variants of this pattern. Anger is triggered without hesitation in nearly 25% of these drivers, with a sizeable number of this group remaining angry following the perceived provocation. The following prescriptions may prove useful.

- ✓ Relax your constant, ever-pressing need to be on guard against other motorists by using positive imagery and other stress management techniques.

- ✓ Visualize a peaceful scene, such as a road winding up to the mountaintop, with no vehicles in sight for miles and miles.

✓ Lessen the hostile affect experienced by the actions of other motorists by exercising more personal control of emotions through constructive self-talk. Verbalize the negative consequences of your potentially irrational behaviors.

✓ Practice direct ways of controlling anxiety by adapting constructive responses, such as backing off, rather than feeling the need to react to intrusive behaviors.

✓ Concentrate on safe driving behaviors and practice relaxation exercises, such as deep breathing whenever you find yourself being provoked by other motorists.

✓ Redirect angry impulses toward other motorists, for example, by hitting a car seat cushion or simply pulling over to the side of the road to relax your tensions and clear your mind.

In Summary

This chapter discussed the behavior of the cynical driver, a skeptical, defensive, and guarded individual. The cynical pattern can range from safe, normal vigilance to neurotic suspiciousness, with various driving behaviors expressed accordingly. These drivers stubbornly guard their personal space and are hypersensitive toward others' perceived "indiscretions." This pattern normally maintains a cautious and cynical style that can quickly turn sarcastic and resentful when slighted.

These motorists will react aggressively toward drivers through direct or indirect expression. Unlike the cautious and guarded approach of the cynical driver, for whom driving requires one's fullest attention, the sociable driver, discussed in the following chapter, is customarily distractible and inattentive on the road, but nevertheless, gregarious and agreeable toward others.

Self Tune-up

Learn to recognize when your thinking is "going the wrong way." Look at the immediate task and approach it optimistically rather than pessimistically. Too many details will confound your concentration and cloud your mind. Focus on the task at hand, e.g., merging on the expressway, parking your car. Rather than wrestling with the details, look at the big picture. Simply think positively, and relax your guard. Drive your mind toward a relaxing destination and enjoy the ride.

---

❻ The Sociable Pattern

Affability and interpersonal relatedness are the hallmarks of the majority of individuals characterized by this style. A search for adventure in life, if not uninhibited excitement, guides this individual on the road. The sociable driver, as its name implies, is a cheerful, pleasant, and friendly motorist who enthusiastically brightens the lives of others. The following features distinguish this style.

- Gregarious and friendly toward other drivers

- Energetic about immediate pursuits

- Frequent use of the rearview mirror, though infrequently uses it for viewing other vehicles

- Prefers spontaneity

- Becomes easily bored on a long stretch of highway

- Easily becomes hurt and may throw a tantrum when other motorists seem "uncooperative"

- At times, exceeds the speed limit for no particular reason

- Emotional disposition can shift rapidly

- Often acts impulsively without considering the consequences of behavior

- Enjoys being noticed by others on the road

Drivers having this style are outgoing, typically charming and amiable with whomever they cross paths. Optimistic about life in general, these upbeat individuals perceive the proverbial half glass of water to be half-full. Having a buoyant spirit, they channel their energy toward living life to its fullest. Each excursion is a novel adventure, with new people and experiences always encountered. Instead of rushing about the roads frenetically, they rather journey excitedly in their pursuit of adventure. They project a high energy level, reacting energetically to external stimulation. In observing this style, their smiles are infectious, bringing goodwill to another motorist's day. As a matter of course, they figuratively, and at times literally, "bump into people," while ingratiating themselves to whomever they meet. In some respects they are chameleon-like, as their moods often change much like the colors of a chameleon, adjusting and adapting to the social situational stage on which they find their specific audience.

Sociable individuals, for the most part, are outgoing and fun-loving people to whom others normally gravitate. Their experiences are alive with vigor. The enthusiasm and exuberance that the sociable style exudes often is contagious. They seek new and exciting challenges and quickly become bored with a humdrum, routine existence. Ever endearing themselves to others, they want to be noticed. They passionately share their zest for life. For the sociable personality, life is adventurous and fully lived, not merely tolerated and endured.

68

Driving Persona

These drivers often garner a cheery wave or smile from passing motorists. On the road, their striking appearance is clearly and immediately evident not only with regard to their emotional response, but also through the vehicles they normally drive. Cruising along on a warm summer day in a flashy convertible, for example, is the prototypical image this pattern commonly conveys. In addition, memories of the carefree college undergrad heading to the Florida beaches for semester break might well describe the expected nature of this individual—a personality that retains youthful charm and craves adventure. These are individuals for whom life's activities, to include driving, are enjoyable and entertaining, rather than taxing and tedious. Though normally positive in their pursuits, they are not necessarily immune to experiencing the travails life has to offer. Yet, when life dishes out lemons, they characteristically make lemonade, paying little heed to surrounding gloom. To cope with another motorist's insensitivity on the road, for example, these drivers may resort to reprogramming their speed-dialing numbers or snapping a quick photo on their cells. In so doing, they deflect the negativity and remove themselves from the "dark room" where negativism develops.

Behavioral reactions, though, are often excessive and dramatic, with a tendency to shift gears unexpectedly. They seek excitement and novelty in life, though generally become disinterested with routine tasks, tiring easily with activities that they do not find stimulating. One may find these individuals speeding along, lost in cell phone conversation and most likely oblivious to the menacing traffic around them. Unconcerned, for instance, about the fuel gauge that may read south of "E" on their panel, these individuals gleefully continue motoring down the highway, absorbed in the moment. They prefer to hear the remainder of their passenger's story before stopping to fill the near-empty gas tank. Conversation with passengers, texting, and self-grooming predictably take precedence over concentrating on the traffic. The following anonymous story sums up this style's behavior regardless of gender.

> Talk about doing everything but driving. Women! On my way to work this morning in bumper-to-bumper traffic, I peered to my left and there's a woman in a Lexus crawling about five miles per hour with her face nearly scrunched into the rearview mirror, attempting to evenly apply her eyeliner. Sheesh! Before I knew it, she's drifting into my lane. I was so distracted. I misdialed my cell and nearly dropped the shaver into my cup of latte!

These drivers don't necessarily disregard safety, rather, they react to an urge of unbridled passion directing them to do what feels good and natural. Youthful stimulus-seeking behaviors guide them through life. Even with maturity, their behaviors may reflect bygone school days, happier times in their past when they were not weighed down by the woes of the world. Nearly 81% state that they

70

are more cautious than other motorists, though males appear slightly more cautious than females. Their outgoing demeanor usually garners attention from others, providing them with the "props" they typically seek. When stranded with engine problems or a flat tire along the side of the road, for example, these individuals soothe their anxieties by knowing that help is only a "smile away," worrying little about their present predicament.

For this pattern, driving is not so much perceived as a necessary means of conveyance, as it is an occasion, a going out in public, so to speak. These drivers decry anonymity on the road because they want and expect to be noticed. Their expressive dramatic style demands that they be recognized. Sociable drivers prefer to use the middle lane, traveling with the flow of traffic for maximum safety. The majority representing this pattern usually drive at a reasonable speed, within five to ten miles over the posted speed limit. Males usually exceed these parameters slightly more than their female counterparts. With respect to safety and caution, slightly more than 50% of the females, as opposed to 90% of the males, believe they are better drivers than are other motorists. As a matter of course, these individuals normally view driving as an appropriate time to "catch up" on other things, such as texting and returning calls. Characteristically distractible, sociable drivers have fleeting attention, and when pressed with unanticipated agitation, such as a sad or distressing phone conversation, tend to lose focus.

Speaking of cell phones, have you ever waited behind a driver who thinks red lights at traffic signals are the opportune time to make a call? What about the cell phone driver in the left lane who is more concerned about the call than the flow of traffic? These behaviors surely are annoyances, but also can be hazardous on the road. Beyond the research suggesting that full attention to driving is gravely restricted when one is engaged in conversation on the cell phone, the underlying question remains, "Shouldn't these activities be entirely banned while driving?" Researchers have determined that a driver's use of a mobile phone up to ten minutes before a crash was associated with a fourfold increased likelihood of crashing, and using a hands-free phone is not any safer than holding the phone.[13] Regrettably, in light of such research, no states ban all cell phone use while driving, though more states are banning texting. Despite local laws, countless drivers continue to use cell phones while driving. Whether their use should be considered contributory negligence in accident cases will remain an issue. Lawmakers believe that hands-free accessories, such as Bluetooth headsets, are the solution. On the contrary, advocates of hands-free cell phone laws fail to comprehend that hands-free cell phone usage does not resolve the problem. As research suggests, using a hands-free phone is not any safer than holding the phone. Moreover, the content of the conversation is equally, if not more, distracting. In fact, the intensity, degree, and content of a typical conversation measurably increase distractibility.

The following narrative clearly illustrates its impact.

Mitchell boarded his Blazer armed with a briefcase in one hand and the ubiquitous cell phone in the other. Cindy, his wife of ten years, nestled into her usual passenger seat, clutching her coffee. They normally drove downtown together to spend "quality time" as a couple, however, on most mornings the conversation usually leads to an intense argument. That is why Mitchell has his cell phone at hand, opportunely managing to make a call whenever he feels the tension build. Usually the call is to his broker—getting pre-market quotes.

On this particular cold morning in February, he dialed his broker as he began "feeling the heat." Nevertheless, as the conversation with his broker grew in intensity, so did his vehicle's rate of speed, with rush hour traffic extremely light at 6:30 in LA. As Cindy sipped her coffee, she slowly began to steam. She glanced at the speedometer and it read 70—then 78! As Mitchell veered to avoid a motorist switching lanes, he sideswiped a state trooper positioned just off the apron and eventually came to rest about a hundred yards beyond the cruiser.

As the trooper walked up to the Blazer, he checked to see if anyone was hurt. The officer noticed that both Mitchell and Cindy were visibly shaken, though no serious injury was apparent. At that point, the trooper noticed the phone in Mitchell's hand and proceeded to deliver a safety lecture on cell phone usage. Cindy, who never used the phone while driving, added that she could not agree more with the officer. She stated that as her husband grew angrier with his broker, their vehicle's speed increased accordingly. She was adamant about Mitchell's cell phone use while driving, but

> Mitchell just waved her off as he usually does when he knows she is right. The Dow was down 844 points that morning.

With this pattern, as with other personality styles, when using cell phones or reading a text message while driving, neither the skill of the driver nor the use of hands-free equipment can insure safety on the road. Distraction from cell phone use while driving (hand-held or hands-free) extends a driver's reaction as much as having a blood alcohol concentration at the legal limit of .08 percent.[14]

The sociable pattern comprised nearly 18% of the individuals surveyed, the second largest group of drivers measured. A slight majority of sociable motorists prefer driving light trucks, with a number choosing to breeze along in a stylish, midsized vehicle, some of which may likely be convertibles.

Vehicle Model Preferences for the Sociable Pattern

Luxury Sedan	12%
Midsized	30%
Compact	24%
Light Truck	31%
Other	03%

With regard to vehicle color, primary-colored vehicles are overwhelmingly chosen by these individuals. With an expressive and outgoing demeanor, intended to gain attention from others, they typically expect to be noticed amid the anonymity. Their vehicles are likely to be flashy in model as well as in color, reflecting their demeanor. These individuals evoke confidence through their dress and appearance as well as the vehicles they drive.

Color Preferences for the Sociable Pattern

White	23%
Earth Tones	19%
Primary Colors	42%
Black	11%
Other	05%

Rage on the Road

Being outwardly expressive with their feelings and occasionally effusive, this individual's mood readily comes to the fore, be it joy or anger. Mood, though, can ebb and flow, depending on the situation. Although gregarious individuals are normally easygoing, their disposition, at times, can turn unpredictable. Irritable feelings can surface, particularly when intentionally "snubbed" by a rude or spiteful motorist. Emotional outbursts, however, are normally short-lived and fleeting. Yet in their "thirst for life," these individuals can become overly distractible, particularly when annoyed, causing them to dramatically veer from the straight and narrow road.

When these individuals become overly excited, they can engage in reckless and uncontrolled behavior. At such times, a manic-like quality displayed through a dramatic expression of emotion comes to the fore. Self-indulgent behaviors can become the focus, as these individuals have a penchant for immediate gratification. Temperament may also become unpredictable, for instance, when these drivers find themselves spontaneously "shifting gears."

With an abrupt display of emotion, parallels can be drawn to the histrionic personality pattern, a variant of the style that is capricious in emotional expressiveness. While the sociable driver may appear outwardly captivating and gregarious, when underlying urges surface, "anger may be expressed as a tantrum or tirade or take the form of a chronic complainer and whiner." [15] The fleeting, changeable mood of this variant is noticeably observed when criticized or challenged, demonstrating expressively rash and uncontrolled behavior at a moment's notice. Their anger, though intense, is short-lived.

Stress-Free Driving Rx

The percentage of drivers in this group who remain angry following a frustrating occurrence is merely 5%. Rarely would this personality initiate road rage behaviors. The incidence among sociable drivers remaining upset is extremely low when compared to other styles. For the most part, these individuals are cheerful and perceived as not having a care in the world. Although gregarious and easygoing, the sociable driver's temperament can turn unpredictable, with anger surfacing on occasion. When negative emotions arise, the following prescriptions may prove helpful.

✓ Identify environmental and occupational stressors. Explore practical techniques of coping with external conditions you cannot change.

✓ Practice direct ways of controlling anxiety by adapting constructive responses, such as moving away from assertive drivers, rather than feeling intimidated.

✓ Reduce the number of emotional urges by pausing a moment to consider the rationale of your actions in relation to other motorists.

✓ Redirect negative impulses toward other motorists by punching the seat cushion or slapping the dashboard to release tension.

✓ Curb inconsistent attitudes by considering alternate courses of action, for example, eliminate distractions, such as cell phone usage while driving.

✓ Pace yourself in life, as well as in traffic.

In Summary

In this chapter, we have reviewed the gregarious cheerful driver who can aptly be described as the friendliest driver on the road. Having extroverted styles, these drivers display their emotions openly, whether expressing joy or anger. When expressions of anger do occur, they are likely fleeting and short-lived, with a rapid return to their sociable and friendly demeanor.

Although many of these drivers are normally safe and cautious, finding them engaged in conversation on a cell phone rather than minding the traffic is not uncommon. They exude confidence in their dress and appearance as well as their driving styles and are gracious and amicable toward other motorists. Unlike the energized, outgoing driver portrayed in this chapter, we turn now to the opposite end of the spectrum, the dispirited personality.

Self Tune-up

When you are tense, breathing is shallow and rapid, and normally occurs in the upper chest. Diaphragmatic Breathing, on the other hand, is deep and rhythmic. This method, also known as abdominal breathing, can be used as a "rapid relaxer." When stressful situations occur on the road, slowly begin to inhale through your nose for approximately a count of five. You will feel your stomach extending as you inhale. Then slowly and evenly exhale through your mouth for approximately another count of five. Practice this procedure, repeating it several times until a relaxed state is achieved.

❼ The Dispirited Pattern

Lacking the verve and energy of the sociable style, the dispirited pattern is described as an insecure, inconsistent, and despondent driving style. Some are erratic drivers, who may feel, at times, detached from the environment. Others are weary and sluggish, giving their "all" simply to remain in the flow of traffic. The following behaviors are suggestive of the dispirited style.

- Occasionally cries for no particular reason

- Frustrated by even minor setbacks

- Becomes anxious in traffic jams

- Worries about personal problems while on the road

- Exaggerated fears of becoming involved in a motor vehicle accident

- Feels fatigued before setting out to drive

- Habitually calls in sick to work

- Experiences feelings of being "taken advantage of" on the road

- Maintains a pessimistic view of life

- Perceived as an unsafe driver

- Has difficulty getting a good night's rest

Everyone, on occasion, feels sad or blue. Usually this frame of mind occurs following some unpleasant event, such as losing a job or separation from a loved one. Sometimes, though, there is no clear reason for this feeling. Dispirited individuals, however, normally feel sad and lethargic much of the time, with some likely experiencing various forms of depression. For the dispirited individual, simply getting out of bed in the morning becomes a strenuous task, much less actually dressing and driving to a job. Concentration and attention difficulties are recurrent, as even the slightest problems become magnified burdens.

Dispirited individuals usually view, as well as relate to the world, through distorted negative self-evaluations. They rarely consider themselves "good-enough" in an ever-demanding world. This distorted view unfortunately serves as a self-fulfilling prophecy of failure by reinforcing, strengthening, and perpetuating an already depressed mood. For some, it is a long-standing pattern of negative self-thoughts and depressed emotion. As Millon notes, "Unlike dysthymia, where episodic patterns of depression are characterized by duration, the depressive pattern uniquely suggests a sustained and continuous condition." [16]

A diminished sense of pleasure in life, feelings of cheerlessness and a sense of hopelessness characterize the dispirited driver. "It has been said that depression is the equivalent of the common cold in psychopathology."[17] Although everyone is seemingly afflicted from time to time, the levels of severity and degree differ with each individual, as well as the situational circumstances. It is normal, for instance, to feel sadness after the death of a spouse or following a divorce or separation. Grieving is a normal emotion, and everyone, we dare say, has experienced it at one time or another. Imagine how you felt during your drive home from the office immediately after you learned that you were fired, or how you felt while driving in the funeral cortege of your late spouse. For the adjusted person, adaptive coping behaviors are summoned to allay the dreadful feelings during such difficult times. Sad and dejected though we may be, these occasions produce normal grieving cycles, and most people work through the eventual suffering and grief. Some surely become stronger following a distressing experience.

When determining the gravity of the depressive condition, the intensity, duration, and strength of the manifested symptoms are measured. Situational grieving and bouts of sadness is a common experience following a traumatic loss, but if one's grief is unresolved and leads to prolonged clinical depression, it easily can become quite disruptive, if not destructive.

Driving Persona

On the road, these individuals are pensive, usually "lost in their own melancholic thought." Most troubling, though, is the risk they can pose to other motorists as well as themselves. These individuals often appear as if they are driving on "autopilot," not fully attuned to the traffic surrounding them. Self-absorbed in their own condition, these individuals are painfully aware of the weight of their burdens. Rearview mirrors seemingly are little more than ornaments in their vehicles, serving no practical safety or cosmetic purpose. For the dispirited driver, quite often, too much energy is simply required to monitor the flow of traffic.

The dispirited individual's energy level resembles that of a cold engine trying to turn over on a frigid wintry morning, such that a good deal of exertion is required simply to "get started." These drivers appear "detached" from the other motorists, even in heavy traffic. Because of accompanying lethargy, cognitive faculties necessary for processing decisions are additionally strained. Their hesitation and indecisiveness are most conspicuous to other motorists, and their inability to concentrate oftentimes creates frustration for those around them. Lack of attention by these drivers can present a dilemma, if not a clear danger, to other motorists. Inattentiveness and lack of concentration on the road usually lead to unexpected and uncertain occurrences.

Interestingly, more than 80% of the dispirited individuals, however, report that they are more cautious in relation to other motorists, though medication may be responsible for this perception. The majority of this group prefers to drive in the right lane with the flow of traffic for maximum safety, although they vary their speed. The preponderance (80%) of both genders representing this pattern drive within ten miles of the posted speed limit. Females exceed these limits slightly more often than do their male counterparts.

Apparently aware of their limited driving ability, merely 50% of this group admits to being better drivers than other motorists, with a 2:1 ratio of males to females. Younger drivers, however, appear to place greater confidence in their driving ability than do older motorists. More than 15% of this group tends to remain angry following an annoyance on the road. These personalities, nevertheless, are habitually absorbed in their own distressing condition, and depending on the degree and intensity of the condition, driving skills are correspondingly diminished.

Vehicle Model Preferences for the Dispirited Pattern

Luxury Sedan	12%
Midsized	22%
Compact	34%
Light Truck	28%
Other	04%

The dispirited pattern comprised nearly 9% of the individuals surveyed (perhaps the percentage of this group may be slightly higher when taking into consideration situational depression), equally split between males and females. Middle-aged motorists, as may be expected, comprise nearly 50% of this group. Dispirited drivers prefer compact cars, perhaps because of fuel efficiency.

With regard to vehicle color, earth tones, suggesting a passive subdued disposition, are clearly the preferred choice of dispirited drivers. The tendency toward softer hues may likely be consistent with their somber and staid temperament.

<u>Color Preferences for the Dispirited Pattern</u>

White	15%
Earth Tones	42%
Primary Colors	26%
Black	15%
Other	02%

Rage on the Road

Several factors, to include environmental, biological, and genetics, contribute to an increased risk for clinical depression. For some, chronic unresolved stressors can increase its risk. Depression may also arise from a chemical imbalance, a biologically-based condition that may be linked to abnormal levels of neurotransmitters. Because of this disorder, one can be much more susceptible to annoyances on the road. Again, the emotional disposition may be environmentally-based, rendering the individual increasingly saddened and melancholic. When a prolonged depressive condition remains untreated, however, the discharge of underlying impulses, specifically unresolved anger, normally occurs. Anger and depression are closely linked, fueling each other with expressed negative affect. Within this pattern, findings suggest an association with the aggressive pattern, perhaps underlining a destructive desire through which aggression is turned against the self. If the dispirited drivers lack energy, how are they able to express aggression? How can a lethargic and sluggish driver muster the strength required to be outwardly confrontational?

Research suggests that suppressed anger underlies depressive conditions. "Patients with masked depression are almost, without exception, extremely angry individuals. The rage could either be overt or covert. In most instances, it was overt."[18] As mentioned, 15% of the individuals comprising this group tend to remain angry following an annoyance on the road, a relatively high percentage among all patterns surveyed. Underlying the depression, however, lurks a seething cauldron of anger and resentment, and frequently the underlying aggressive feelings are masked through a depressive *persona*. It has been said that depression is "anger turned inward." More than 17 million Americans suffer from depression,[19] and without proper prescribed medication, these numbers may likely add to the number of aggressive drivers on the road. While certain medications can reduce the intensity of the symptoms, some self-medication, to include alcohol, serves to exacerbate an already unstable condition. It is important to note here that some antidepressants can significantly impair judgment, concentration, and overall driving performance, while others can cause a severe state of anxiety. The interaction of antidepressants and alcohol greatly diminishes perception and coordination on the road, and when combined, are effectively lethal weapons when driving. Although most depressive individuals likely receive proper medication to ease their symptoms, driving while medicated or under the influence is too often a major safety concern on today's highways. The following vignette highlights the actual difference between normal grieving and clinical depression, a line insidiously crossed by some. Additionally, it punctuates the tenuous fragility of the normal individual psyche.

> Two years ago, friends and family came together to celebrate Jenny and Frank's golden wedding anniversary. Frank proudly acknowledged at the banquet that Jenny was his "whole world." In more ways than one that was true. She cooked, cleaned, and paid all the bills, and, most important, she was a devoted wife. Despite that Frank's health had been declining over the past few years, he was grateful to have a wife who lovingly and willingly took care of him. Jenny made life worth living.
>
> Six months ago, however, friends and family gathered once again—this time to pay their final respects to Jenny, who had suffered a fatal heart attack. Frank was suddenly alone. To make matters worse, he had relied on Jenny for everything—even basic survival. As a result of losing her, Frank neglected himself as well as his home and his life.
>
> To escape the memories and relieve the grief, Frank turned to alcohol. Empty bottles of vodka were usually strewn across his living room floor. Frank was despondent. He would regularly take the car out for midnight drives, swerving his way through

the streets to his destination—the liquor store in the next town. Alcohol was his only solace. Needless to say, his perception was usually distorted. He had many near misses, but one night, his luck ran out.

On his way home, he felt a thud on the dark road and assumed that he hit a deer. He was too inebriated to stop to check what had happened. Although he somehow made it home, the police soon arrived at his house. Frank had struck a teen walking home with a friend after a graduation party. The stress of the accident worsened Frank's health problems and he became more depressed. Guilt wholly consumed him. Although the young man survived, he would also be permanently disabled. The thought of that haunted Frank, and he decided that he would try to make it up to the young victim.

One night, Frank took his car out for the last time. His car struck a cement barrier on the expressway and he was killed instantly. Weeks before, he had taken out a large insurance policy with the young disabled teen listed as the beneficiary, thinking he would assuage his guilt.

Suicidal, Frank had bungled his last act of desperation. Ironically, no one benefited. Frank inevitably chose the route of "Willy Loman" as his only way out.

How many dispirited drivers additionally self-medicate with alcohol, compounding their condition? Is not alcohol considered by some to be a convenient and inexpensive elixir to ease one's burden? Alcohol, itself a depressant, exacerbates and compounds a depressive condition, and as we clearly know, driving under the influence remains a major problem on our roads. As Frank's behavior testifies, the literature is rife with statistics regarding the inappropriate use of alcohol and driving fatalities. According to data from the National Highway Traffic Safety Administration (NHTSA), 37,261 people died in traffic crashes in 2008 in the United States with DUI driving fatalities accounting for 32% of all traffic deaths. [20]

Frank clearly crossed the line from reactive mourning to clinical depression. Unfortunately, he turned to self-medication through alcohol to deaden the inexpressible grief in his life. Alcohol, ironically, only heightened his desperation, rather than offer relief. Symptoms of depression, though, are not always as intense as Frank's. Signs and symptoms vary in intensity and duration from one person to the next. Its diagnosis can range from mild, chronic symptoms of dysthymia to major depressive episodes, as experienced by Frank.

Much of the experienced anger and expressed aggression when turned inward, though, can result in self-destructive behaviors, such as Frank's suicide on the road. How many "accidents" recorded in our country are actually masked suicides? How many DUI "accidents" are actually related to suicide? Although the majority of motor vehicle collisions are recorded as accidents, one must question what portion of these are intentional suicides. Is there a link between unconscious suicidal motivations and automobile accidents? Research of fatal accidents suggests that some of the deaths attributed to vehicular accidents may result from suicidal intent. "The risk of an injurious crash was significantly increased for those drivers who reported to have previous or current suicidal ideation but without current antidepressant medication."[21] It appears that the characteristics of the dispirited personality might comprise, at least in part, a percentage of the drivers in this category.

Stress-Free Driving Rx

Many situations in life, as suggested, can generate depressed feelings. Certain conditions, whether biologically, genetically, or environmentally based, however, make some individuals more prone to develop the varied symptoms of depression. Notably, the severity and impairment varies with the individual. Severity and degree of the condition, as well as other personal factors, most assuredly determine the driver's ability to operate a motor vehicle safely.

Modifying one's environment to meet one's needs is normal behavior. For the depressed individual, though, coping maneuvers often prove futile. The depressed individual usually views and relates to the world through distorted negative self-evaluations, and being so perceived, the distorted view of self is too often "verified" in reality. A feedback loop inevitably develops, thereby setting into motion a string of self-defeating sequences that strengthen and perpetuate an already depressed mood. The following prescriptions may prove beneficial for these individuals.

- ✓ Most importantly, if you find yourself in a melancholic mood, particularly if you use alcohol or prescribed medication to soothe your sadness, recognize that you are physically impaired—and by all means, curb your automobile.

89

✓ Decrease frequent worrisome thoughts by adopting thought-stopping measures by simply saying to yourself, "Stop!" Repeated interruptions can help eliminate stressful, unwanted thoughts.

✓ Attempt to normalize your stress. Be patient and "understanding" of your condition. Putting together positive coping strategies takes time. Remember to break larger, unmanageable tasks into smaller, more "do-able" tasks.

✓ Explore underlying feelings of negative self-worth and self-esteem. Challenge the futility of harboring these feelings. Create a list of strengths and appropriate response behaviors on which you can rely.

✓ Replace negatively directed thoughts (I can't do it), with positively directed thoughts (I can do it).

✓ Above all, learn to relax when tensions mount. Let go of daily stressors by softly repeating words of comfort, e.g., "I am calm and relaxed," as you imagine yourself slowly ascending a beautiful marble staircase leading to a peaceful, serene haven.

✓ If depressive symptoms become unmanageable, seek therapeutic help. Consult your physician.

In Summary

This chapter discussed the dispirited driver, a depressed individual, characteristically melancholic and dissatisfied with many areas of life. Everyone, on occasion, feels sad or blue. Dispirited individuals, on the other hand, normally feel sad and lethargic much of the time and are likely diagnosed with some form of depression. The depressed person bottles up anger, and largely represses painful negative emotion. This experience can be like sitting on a powder keg. Based on individual personality, the negative emotion can be aggressively directed toward self or others when ignited. Of all the styles studied, the dispirited style correlated most positively with the aggressive pattern. Before discussing the aggressive driver, let us first turn to the timid pattern.

Self Tune-up

A strategy known as "thought stopping" [22] can prove useful when applied to angry situations. As you find yourself starting to lose your temper, and negativity is about to take hold of you, saying "Stop!" may prove helpful in initially diffusing your anger. When you find yourself feeling negative about yourself or another motorist, take a deep breath, then imagine a large red blinking light and again say the word "Stop!" to yourself. Replace the negative thoughts with positive thinking.

If the negative thoughts persist, begin wearing a rubber band around your wrist. When angry feelings take hold, simply snap the rubber band to make you aware of the negative affect you are experiencing. Then again replace the negativity with positive thoughts.

If depressive symptoms become debilitating, consult your physician.

---

❽ The Timid Pattern

Because of an underlying sensitivity to social rejection, timid drivers distance themselves from others. Timid drivers are unsure of themselves, unusually fearful of what they might encounter on the road. Notwithstanding the sense of anonymity that driving on a highway produces, these motorists subject themselves to the scrutiny of others. The following identifying characteristics describe the timid personality.

- Prefers others to do the driving

- Shy and distant toward others

- Fears criticism

- Usually anxious behind the wheel

- Maintains a greater than normal distance between vehicles

- Perceived as an unskilled driver

- Overly cautious, particularly when traffic is congested

- Displays deference toward other motorists

- Unfailingly obeys the rules of the road

- Rarely, if ever, engages in risky driving behaviors

- Lacks self-esteem

- Keenly aware of surrounding environment

The timid personality is characterized by a pattern of withdrawal, inadequacy, and extreme sensitivity to criticism. Avoidance is the dominant feature of this personality because of an underlying fear of rejection. Regarding the timid driver, as the pattern suggests, one finds an individual who is self-conscious and apprehensive, the most tentative of driving styles on the road. Except for the aggressive pattern, the timid driver is the most easily recognizable style on the road. They are usually tense and apprehensive on the road, unable to make speedy decisions, particularly in heavy traffic. An awkwardness, uneasiness, and reticence characterize this anxious personality behind the wheel. Unsure of their ability, these individuals tend to shy away from congested traffic areas, preferring to avoid expressway driving entirely.

Consider the individual who appears "lost" on the roadways, not with regard to geographical location, but because of a tense uneasiness in operating the vehicle. Undoubtedly, a timid driver is likely driving. Accounts of individuals applying the accelerator instead of the brakes are normal occurrences, and possibly the result of hesitancy, anxiety, and indecision demonstrated by this style of motorist. Unassertive and apprehensive on the road, as well as in their daily lives, they rarely take risks. Ironically, life itself is perceived as a risk, as they venture out seemingly "unequipped" to face the world. An overall fear of inadequacy is the cornerstone of this style and leads to poor decision-making behaviors. Easily overcome with stress, driving is an anxiety producing, if not challenging activity. This individual is pressured with anxiety and only fully at ease on the road when someone else is behind the wheel. This pattern displays a distinct propensity toward social introversion, presenting overly cautious traits and expressly apprehensive behavior on the road and in life.

Driving Persona

Timid drivers comprised approximately 13% of the sample respondents. They are shy, withdrawn, and reserved in public as well as on the road. Though these individuals approach the road with much trepidation, for the most part, they are careful drivers. They comply with the rules of the road and are sensitive to other motorists. Rarely would these individuals use a cell phone while driving, since fullest attention to driving is required. The majority of this group prefers driving in the middle lane with the flow of traffic. Rarely does this individual travel at excessive speeds, with the majority of drivers (nearly 80%) remaining within five miles per hour of the posted speed limit. This group, as may be expected, drives at the slowest rates of speed among all personality patterns. Speeding motorists normally pass these individuals from all angles, further heightening their anxiety behind the wheel.

Timid drivers believe that they are less skilled than other motorists, both in operating the vehicle, as well as understanding the nuances of driving. Increased traffic, poor weather, and speeding motorists only serve to heighten their apprehension. As traffic density increases, so does their stress. These individuals are acutely aware of the hazards on the road, typically satisfied, and thankful, to simply arrive safely at their destination. They give others the impression that they are in a world of their own, almost removed expressively from the task at hand, and at times, appearing to be muddling along in an undaunted fashion. Nothing, however, can be further from the truth. In fact, they become overly tense and anxious when drawn too close to others, and instinctively retreat. Timid individuals consciously avoid any hint of conflict. In the face of confrontation extreme anxiety may "paralyze" these drivers into inaction, leaving them perplexed. The "deer in the headlights" stare most accurately describes this individual behind the wheel. The following story exemplifies the timid driver when confronted with an anxiety-producing situation.

Judy is a business owner, running a school uniform company. Because of her job, she logged quite a few miles behind the wheel of her Nissan Maxima.

A single and independent individual, she never thought that one day she would almost "lose her head" over a man, that is, until she met Bob.

One day during the height of the late afternoon rush hour, Bob was stuck in traffic. Bob was an overly cautious driver—perhaps a bit too cautious. He looked around, fearing being hit by another motorist at any given moment. He tapped his fingers on the steering wheel, but it was no use. Crawling inch by inch with his Ford Focus, his anxiety continued to mount.

96

Eventually, the momentum of the traffic provided a long-awaited break between vehicles, and Bob decided to exit at the first opportunity. With a white-knuckle grasp on the wheel, he cringed as he attempted to maneuver his vehicle into the far-right lane. Cars honked as he finally positioned himself closer to the exit ramp and carefully accelerated. The car in front of him belonged to Judy.

Judy's car came to an abrupt halt because the vehicle in front of her stalled. Bob inadvertently applied pressure to the gas pedal instead of the brakes this time and sure enough, Bob rammed his vehicle into Judy's.

What he witnessed at that point horrified him. He saw a head jerk with such force that he could swear it flew into the back seat of the Maxima. "Good grief, I think I've decapitated her!" He was momentarily paralyzed, but managed to jump out of his car to look into Judy's vehicle.

On the floor was Judy, all right. She was leaning over, but to his relief, she was there trying to retrieve her big, bouffant wig from the back seat!

Bob's lack of confidence in his driving ability contributed to his anxiety and rendered him unable to handle the added pressure. As expected, such situations can create a modicum of confusion as well as anguish for fellow motorists. For example, when instant acceleration is required to safely merge with the flow of expressway traffic, this individual may hesitate or inappropriately apply the brake. The motorists following, must then exercise vigilance, not to mention a good deal of patience. Accustomed to distancing themselves in life as well as on the road, they prefer a larger than normal space between vehicles. In so doing, they create added stress by having a stream of vehicles continually filling it. Regarding choice of vehicles, females prefer to drive midsize sedans while males opt for compacts or light trucks.

Vehicle Model preferences for the Timid Pattern

Luxury Sedan	12%
Midsized	31%
Compact	27%
Light Truck	26%
Other	04%

Nearly 40% of this group opts for a primary-colored vehicle. Typically lacking in social judgment skills and besought with feelings of inadequacy, timid individuals typically have little confidence in themselves and their driving ability. Primary-colored vehicles would not necessarily suggest the shy retiring demeanor of these drivers, however opting for a loud outgoing color may serve to bolster their reserved disposition.

Color Preferences for the Timid Pattern

White	18%
Earth Tones	30%
Primary Colors	39%
Black	09%
Other	04%

Rage on the Road

Timid individuals are the least likely of all personality styles to exhibit any sort of aggressive outbursts, with outward expression of anger being exceedingly rare. For the most part, when negative emotion surfaces, urges are quickly harnessed and usually directed inwardly. These individuals normally hold themselves responsible for the effects of their negative emotion. Of all the drivers identified as timid, a slight percentage tended to remain angry following an irritable incident on the road. For example, when timid individuals attempt to parallel-park on a narrow street and the moving vehicle behind them prohibits this action by invading the necessary space required, timid drivers will unassumingly move to another space. These drivers show no tendency to remain upset, perhaps because of a lack of emotional responsiveness and learned avoidance to frustrating experiences.

For timid drivers, frustrating situations, such as traffic congestion, serves to trigger an internal alarm, setting off increased, and sometimes uncontrollable anxiety. Additionally, they are burdened with the fear that they will act in a way that will be humiliating or embarrassing. Most drivers experience normal anxiety, for instance, when they are unable to change lanes in timely fashion while exiting a crowded expressway. If the driver misses a desired exit, for example, most drivers will safely merge across traffic and subsequently exit at the next available exit. Such a situation for the timid individuals, however, may leave them with feelings of being trapped, resulting in a panic-like reaction. Their inability to extricate themselves from such a situation may leave them sweating profusely, with hands tightly gripped to the steering wheel. The intense anxiety may cripple their adaptive responsiveness, thereby creating further complications for themselves as well as other motorists. All of us have encountered such drivers on the road, for instance, drivers who suddenly accelerate when they should be braking. How many incidents, such as drivers running into fast-food restaurants in Chicago or drivers crashing into baggage counters in San Francisco are blamed on mechanical difficulties? In reality, these mishaps may, perhaps, have been the result of an overly anxious timid driver who suddenly panics at the most inopportune moment. Is it operator error or vehicle malfunction? Though the aggressive pattern, as we expect, is the embodiment of reckless and irresponsible behavior on the road, the timid style, perhaps because of unsettling anxiety, may also at times, pose somewhat of a risk to other motorists.

In examining the driving behavior of timid drivers, this pattern, as mentioned, is the least likely of all styles to exhibit rage on the road. With their cautious style, one would rarely see this style tailgating, driving on a shoulder, or displaying other aggressive behaviors. Confrontation rarely, if ever occurs. As the timid personality withdraws from confrontation, its opposite, the aggressive personality, seeks it. There is a marked difference in attitudes between the cautious timid drivers and careless aggressive drivers in relation to safety. Despite being excessively anxious, timid drivers are among the safer drivers on the road. "The timid drivers will tend to leave a longer space, drive more slowly and be reluctant to change lanes, while an aggressive driver will tend to tailgate, cut-in in front of others, change lanes to overtake on the inside and substantially exceed the speed limit." [23]

Stress-Free Driving Rx

This pattern is not predisposed to remain angry following a disrupting incident on the road. As suggested, timid individuals are the least likely of all personality styles to exhibit any sort of angry outbursts. Timid drivers avoid confrontation, rarely exhibiting any outward aggression. Negative emotion is usually directed inwardly, creating an undercurrent of disruptive internal tension. Underlying the timid personality, however, is a reluctance to take personal risks, primarily for fear of being criticized, embarrassed, or rebuffed. Consequently, these individuals fashion a pattern of social inhibition, developing feelings of inadequacy and discomfort in public settings, to include the highways. To combat this apprehension, they must initially learn to soothe themselves through confident self-appraisal of their established abilities. The following stress-relievers may also prove useful.

✓ Practice maintaining positive body language along with rehearsing appropriate conversational skills and interpersonal behaviors.

✓ Teach yourself to be aware of stressful bodily stimuli, such as sweaty palms. At such times, practice self-relaxation techniques, such as deep breathing exercises.

✓ Identify situations that make you uncomfortable, e.g., feelings of helplessness when you get lost on the highway. Counter these thoughts by saying, for instance, "Getting lost is frustrating, but with my GPS, I will find the location."

✓ Identify situations in which you would like to be more forceful. For example, when people take advantage of you on the expressway, ask yourself how you would like to respond to them and determine which behaviors are appropriate.

✓ Describe a problem-scenario you're experiencing, and then explore appropriate methods of resolution. For example, your carpool friend is always late when picking you up in the morning, causing you to be late for work through no fault of your own. What steps can you take to avoid this anxiety?

✓ Reduce the frequency of negative self-thoughts, for example, "I am a terrible driver, I shouldn't even be on the road," and replace them with positive, reinforcing thoughts, such as, "I am a careful driver. I have been driving for more than ten years and have had no accidents."

In Summary

Being shy, withdrawn, and reserved in public, these individuals approach the road with much trepidation; however, they are among the more careful drivers. While timid drivers are essentially safe and conscientious, their actions can occasionally disrupt the flow of moving traffic and become a source of irritation for the impetuous motorist. Whereas timid drivers may increase the safe distance between vehicles, other individuals on the road, such as aggressive drivers, are quick to fill that space. This creates added anxiety for the timid motorist. Unassertive in their behaviors and unsure of their abilities, the timid driver readily gives way to the other motorists on the road, without any hint of a confrontational attitude. One such driver to whom this driver readily defers is the aggressive driver, who is discussed in the next chapter.

Self Tune-up

When driving on an expressway that may cause anxiety or panic-like symptoms, consider the worse thing that may happen. Imagine yourself trembling and your palms becoming moist. Then let go of those thoughts. Open your window and throw them out.

Collect yourself and take hold of the situation. Relax your forehead and jaws with pressured spiral movements of your fingers. Release the tension around the area. Repeat this exercise several times until the anxiety lessens.

➒ The Aggressive Pattern

When speaking of road rage, the aggressive style is the gold standard by which road rage is measured. As noted throughout, all personalities are capable of expressing aggressive behavior—degree and intensity, however, vary greatly. Yet, some personalities by their very nature are more susceptible to irritability and provocation, and more prone to respond in a hostile and aggressive manner. The identifying characteristics of the aggressive personality are provided.

- Competitive by nature and expects confrontation

- Exhibits reckless driving behaviors

- Takes pleasure in intimidating another driver

- Quick to use the horn when a driver reacts slowly as the red traffic signal turns to green

- Feels that most people take advantage of others

- Engages in reckless behaviors, creating dangerous situations on the road

- Usually high strung, and hypersensitive toward other motorists

- Hard-driving, *type A* personality

- Has little remorse following confrontational behavior on the road

There exists a crystallized and embedded dimension of aggressiveness that permeates every aspect of this driver's behavior. Unlike other patterns that may lash out at other motorists on occasion, the disposition of aggressive individuals is habitually and unaffectedly insensitive, if not outwardly antagonistic. Without a doubt, aggressive actions of other personalities may outwardly resemble this pattern, and on occasion, similarly display aggressive behavior on the road. Although the aggressive actions of other personalities may sometimes resemble this pattern, it is this individual's inflexible and pervasive internal frame of mind, namely, survival through conquest that drives this style and ostensibly distinguishes this driver from other motorists on the road. This personality is competitive by nature, expecting and embracing confrontation. Nevertheless, when describing the aggressive style, a distinction between its variants is in order.

As with the structure of other personality styles, the degree of aggressiveness in this pattern ranges from mild to severe. In milder forms, this individual normally demonstrates a flair for daring adventure, presenting a bold demeanor, with a dynamic focus toward the world. They are usually impatient, particularly toward those who putter along in the fast lane while cradling their cell phones. Obviously driven, these individuals are ambitious, single-minded, and extremely determined in any pursuit, to include driving.

With regard to the milder form, this variant appears

assertive, that is, one who is inherently self-confident, assured, and competitive. Shifting along the continuum, the severe form describes the driver who navigates the highways with reckless abandonment, typically enraged and confrontational. Unconcerned about the welfare of others, this variant is "ready for combat." This forceful *persona* demonstrates a pattern characterized by risk-taking behavioral appearance, intimidating interpersonal conduct, subjective cognitive style, angry affective expression, and an aggressive self-perception.[24] In the extreme, this variant more closely resembles individuals, who by today's standards, exhibit aggressive road rage. This variant displays strikingly aggressive traits, ranging from antagonistic taunts to outright hostility. Without question, there exists a fine line between the assertive and aggressive variants in behavioral terms, and at times, difficult for the untrained observer to differentiate on the road.

Nevertheless, assertive driving reflects a self-confident boldness on the road, marked by competition with others, while the aggressive *persona* fearlessly dominates and bullies others with no concern for their welfare. They resort to aggressive driving simply to defend themselves. "The basic aggressive type dreads the thought of being weak, of being deceived, and of being humiliated. These individuals perceive others' bold actions as affronts, normally blaming the environment for their own failures and inadequacies. Their primary task is to outsmart others, to gain power over them before the others outfox and dominate them." [25] Both variants of the aggressive personality pattern tend to be adventurous, intimidating, and risk-taking drivers. Having a forceful character, these individuals noticeably set themselves apart from others, acting as the "leader of the pack"—at least in their minds!

Driving Persona

The aggressive driver habitually commits multiple offenses on the road—from speeding to tailgating—with impunity. Ever the chronic aggressor, this driver is quick to react to the slightest perceived provocation.

Although many drivers may occasionally become irritated on the road, their expressed anger is much less volatile and noticeably more controlled than the aggressive style. The aggressive driver can be likened to a bully on the road. When these drivers become enraged on the highway, they strike out against others in an aggressive, if not violent, fashion. They not only overreact, but also exercise poor judgment. Their actions, in the extreme, more closely define the notion of road rage as applied to the reckless drivers on the road.

Challenges are embraced rather than eschewed. Competitive and earnest in their undertakings, a *type A* personality pattern is clearly reflected in this individual. The aggressive drivers tolerate few restrictions, ever striving for control as they seek unfettered freedom and dominance on the open roads. These motorists attribute actions, such as racing through a yellow light as it is about to turn red or rolling through a stop sign, to smart and skillful driving. The unbridled aggressiveness of these individuals quickly transforms into rage when impositions are placed on them or challenges made to their freewheeling spirit. Refusing to be intimidated in any pursuit, these individuals strive to enforce self-rule, believing that the rules of the road do not apply to them.

Viewing themselves as nonconformists, they tend to ignore traditional authority, as well as its rules. "If we accept their premise that ours is a dog-eat-dog world, we can understand why they value being so tough, forthright, and unsentimental." [26] These drivers believe other motorists to be the antagonists, actually seeking competition through provocation. Some do not even entertain the thought that their driving style is aggressive. If accused of aggressive driving, they may boldly claim to be protecting their own interests. For example, they may interpret being passed by another motorist as a challenging invitation for competition. Despite their disregard for the rights of others, subjectively they may believe they have done no harm. Anonymity on the road breeds, if not empowers the aggressive expression and conviction of these individuals. Presuming there will be few, if any repercussions, they act with impunity.

The aggressive drivers expect and anticipate hostility from others. As a result, they must "get in the first punch." This pattern refers to an internal disposition as "moving against people," a style that sees the road as an arena, where, in Darwinian terms, only the fittest survive. [27]

Although other patterns, such as the sociable style, are inclined to soothe a confrontational situation, the aggressive style will likely fan the flames of provocation. When other patterns become annoyed with fellow motorists, they often ignore the infraction. The aggressive driver, however, normally takes direct action against the "offending" motorist, perhaps by a gesture or more aggressive action. Regrettably, more often than not, their behaviors are at the expense of others.

Though nearly 80% of drivers in this group maintain a consistent and reasonable speed limit (5-10-mph over the limit), 20% regularly exceed speeds of 20mph beyond the posted limit. The majority of these motorists prefer to travel in the right lane, suggesting that they are, perhaps, "flying under the radar" to avoid detection. Within this group, both males and females travel at the same rate of speed, normally fast. Approximately 75% of all aggressive individuals stated that they wear seatbelts, with 82% signaling their intentions by using directional indicators. Females are apparently more safety conscious than males, scoring in the 90th percentile in these areas. Males, oddly enough, tend to perceive themselves as more cautious than other motorists.

This pattern comprised approximately 9% of the respondents. This percentage may likely reflect the number of aggressive individuals found in the driving public. The preferred model of vehicle for both genders is clearly the light truck, with more than 40% opting for this model.

Vehicle Model Preferences for the Aggressive Pattern

Luxury Sedan	11%
Midsized	23%
Compact	23%
Light Truck	42%
Other	01%

As with the choice of vehicle model, there also exists a clear preference regarding color of vehicle by males as well as females. Black is obviously the color of choice, perhaps suggesting power and confidence on the road.

Color Preferences for the Aggressive Pattern

White	19%
Earth Tones	20%
Primary Colors	16%
Black	40%
Other	05%

Rage on the Road

Our competitive society seemingly endorses and rewards assertive *type A* personalities, as may likely be evidenced in the number of highly motivated "workaholics." Yet, an individual's healthy assertiveness can swiftly become transformed into *Hyde's* unhealthy aggressiveness, and in its extreme form, expressed maladaptively as violent road rage. A dormant quality of the aggressive personality may suddenly surface, changing one's direction.

When transformed, the aggressive pattern takes on antisocial variants of behavior, displaying reckless abandon. In most severe forms these individuals exhibit indifference and an outright lack of concern in their contempt for societal laws as well as fellow motorists. They tend to speed, tailgate, pass on the shoulder, and generally exhibit irresponsible behavior while driving. For the aggressive individual, the vehicle can indeed become a weapon. Unlike other styles that might, on occasion, exhibit aggressive behavior, the rage of the aggressive individual is active rather than reactive, deliberate rather than unplanned.

The antisocial variant of the aggressive style, purely and simply, is the embodiment of rage on the road. "Not only are such individuals seemingly undaunted by danger and punishment, they appear attracted to it, and may actually seek it out and provoke it."[28] These individuals are commonly the sources of road rage. Their rage, though, may be associated with an impulse control disorder, such as Intermittent Explosive Disorder (IED). The disorder may be the result of an imbalance of neurotransmitters, mild neurological abnormalities, or varied environmental factors. According to the DSM-IV, Intermittent Explosive Disorder is an impulse control disorder that is characterized by discrete episodes of failure to resist aggressive impulses resulting in serious assaults. The degree of aggressivenes expressed is grossly out of proportion to any provocation. [29] When challenged on the road, this personality easily becomes enraged, if not vindictive. Expressions of anger are

112

deliberate and violent. Generally, when a motorist comes across such drivers on the road, especially if confronted, common sense dictates that the other motorist should exercise restraint, since the aggressive driver typically seeks confrontation and may inflict harm. The following story relates an incident that occurred on an urban freeway and accurately describes the deadly violence an aggressive individual is capable of inflicting on another.

This Commute is Murder!

Judging from recent news reports, highway fatalities are often the product of road rage. This was certainly the case several months ago, when an electronics worker made the fatal mistake of cutting off an administrative assistant in traffic.

Appropriate gestures were exchanged, prompting an enraged administrative assistant to follow the electronics worker for several miles, staying right on the bumper of her SUV.

She exited eventually, though the other followed. Seething with anger, the two women parked at the edge of the off-ramp whereupon the pursuer, a woman of substantial girth, leaped from her pickup truck and approached the victim's passenger side.

Seeking to reduce the other woman's obvious size advantage, she grabbed a .38 caliber handgun she kept stashed in the vehicle.

Most people would view this as a scare tactic, but she did more than brandish her weapon. According to witnesses, she stuck it out the window of her Toyota 4-Runner and shot the woman point blank in the face.

> She was, a 34-year-old mother of three, who slumped to the pavement, dead. Her neighbors described her as a friendly person who loves dogs and children.
>
> Feeling lucky today? [30]

Such individuals habitually express their aggression directly. As described above, arguments typically escalate rather quickly into physical violence with this style. In such unjustifiable and heated attacks, one's rage is usually uncontrollable and intense. Senseless behavior can happen anywhere, anytime. Impulsivity is evidenced and is often associated with self-damaging behaviors, such as substance abuse, binge drinking, and, of course, reckless driving. Anyone accustomed to driving is all too familiar with the propensity for aggressive driving and knows that these drivers commonly show a pattern of blatant disregard for the rights of others and society in general. They fail to conform to societal norms, engaging in criminal behaviors with perceived impunity. These individuals might give the impression of being non-socialized, seemingly unable to respect others and adjust to social norms. Violations of the law are commonplace and disregard for the rules is routine. Yet, ironically, some aggressive drivers, who have snapped and committed violence on the road, are occasionally successful men and women, with no known histories of crime, violence, or alcohol and drug abuse. In media interviews, for instance, friends and neighbors of these persons give historical accounts, such as, "He is the kindest man, a wonderful father, or he must have been provoked." Marked by hard-driving characteristics, these individuals perceive driving on the road to be a competitive sport. They compete with others as they do with themselves and are seemingly unrelenting in their pursuit to control others. Though the mild variant of this pattern exhibits adaptive assertiveness, this style readily transforms into maladaptive aggressiveness, expressed violently on the road as rage. An intriguing phenomenon, however, exists. Although males normally are perceived as the typical aggressive driver by the general populace, interestingly, the percentage of individual personalities identified as "aggressive" in this survey is nearly equal in gender. The gender gap apparently is closing, particularly in relation to aggressive driving.

Stress-Free Driving Rx

The aggressive pattern, by a wide margin among styles, is most likely to remain angry following an incident on the road. Once engaged, they "fight to the finish." Research suggests that Intermittent Explosive Disorder, observed in certain cases of road rage, affects as many as 7.3 % of adults or 16 million Americans, in their lifetimes.[31] The following individual guidance may prove beneficial.

✓ Minimize perceived slights and abuse from other motorists by "placing yourself in their shoes."

✓ Relax the need to constantly be "on guard" against other motorists. Practice positive imagery and other stress management techniques.

✓ Reduce negative affect experienced toward other motorists by exercising personal restraint through the customary use of socially acceptable behaviors.

✓ If you are noticeably angry and upset regarding issues on a particular day, consider an alternate means of transportation, or ride with someone else that day.

✓ If you find yourself screaming violently at other motorists, pause, take a look at yourself in the rearview mirror, and ask yourself, "Why are you having a childish tantrum?"

✓ Reduce the number of emotional urges by pausing a moment to consider the rationale of your actions versus those of the other motorist.

✓ Gradually reframe ways of defining the environment through positive strategies, such as pulling off to the side of the road when angry impulses begin to surface.

✓ Practice control of emotions and behaviors through stress-reduction techniques, such as deep-breathing or yoga-like exercises when frustrated in traffic.

✓ Understand the ramifications of your actions, and their impact on yourself, as well as others. Adopt appropriate behaviorally framed problem-solving techniques.

✓ Develop an attitude of respect for other drivers. Change your "I don't care" attitude into an "I care" approach toward others.

✓ Consider direct ways of controlling anger, for example, by adopting constructive responses, such as counting to ten before impulsively acting out.

✓ Slow Down!

In Summary

As discussed throughout, though all personality patterns have the capacity for acting on hostile impulses with an occasional display of aggressive driving behavior, this personality style habitually and unaffectedly embraces aggressive driving. Many people become angry while driving, however, the anger of aggressive drivers is clearly out of control. Perhaps the inability to control anger, in some cases, is linked to a chemical imbalance producing intermittent explosive disorder. Yet, it is the degree and intensity of aggressive behavior that distinguishes the aggressive style from all others. These drivers are inflexible and obstinate in their thinking process, needlessly disregarding the safety and well-being of fellow motorists. Their rage is active, rather than reactive, often with the intent to inflict harm.

The aggressive style ranges from mild to severe, with a marked difference evidenced throughout the breadth of its spectrum. The milder forms of aggressiveness exhibit a penchant for adventure and a desire to live on the edge, challenging personal limits and boundaries. This variant may be labeled the bold aggressive—self-confident, assertive, assured, and *type A*. These individuals tend to be impatient and irritable, though less volatile in expressing rage. On the far end of the spectrum, however, is the variant that personifies individuals who engage in violent road rage. This extreme form can be termed the forceful aggressive— intimidating, dominating and dangerous. With the profile of

117

the aggressive driver, we close the presentation of the various personality patterns. In the final chapter, we will examine more closely the dimensions of road rage.

Self Tune-up

When overcome with rage on the road, squeeze the steering wheel as tightly as possible with both hands, grasping it, tighter and harder. Then simply relax! Take one hand and place the tips of your fingers on your temple area, then behind your ears, then around your neck. Massage each area for about 30 seconds— or until your initial anger passes. Repeat the exercise with the other hand to the opposite side of your head.

After you find yourself somewhat relaxed, begin to massage your mind. Imagine yourself driving along a peaceful road, perhaps through a winding pass in the country. Imagine the scene vividly with all your senses. Breathe in the tranquility and taste the stillness of the air, smell the scent of the flowers, and feel the distress slowly leave your muscles. Calmly relax.

---

⑩ Unmasking Road Rage

As most drivers discover, the range of behavioral and emotional attitudes that converge on our nation's highway system are as diverse as the models of vehicles driven today. Individual personality patterns dictate the diversity of driving practices, with each style reacting differently to stressors on the road. Nowhere is this convergence of such divergence as conspicuous and glaring as on our highways.

Throughout the preceding chapters, eight individual personality patterns were presented—roles played out on the road, as well as acted out on the stage of life. It is clear that personality influences the way one thinks, feels, acts, and undeniably, the way one drives. A personality pattern comprised of one's characteristic traits is uniquely and intricately woven within each individual. How one interacts with the environment, how anger is expressed, how one copes with stress, or how aggressively one "acts" on the road is primarily a function of one's embedded personality pattern.

Although the percentage of individuals having a proclivity for aggressive driving is relatively small in relation to the number of drivers on America's highways, everyone is susceptible to aggressive behavior on the road. Furthermore, depending on mood, condition, and situation, any driver, despite personality type, is capable of demonstrating aggressive behavior. Throughout the earlier chapters, it has been underscored that individuals having a maladaptive personality pattern are more prone to act out on the road. Within such personalities, aggressive tendencies are more readily revealed when the *persona* is unmasked *ala Hyde* behind the wheel, oftentimes to the surprise or dismay of the driver. Surely, all personality patterns have the capacity for aggressive behavior and exhibit various degrees of acting out behaviors on the road, but what essentially causes a driver to act out? In other words, what actually triggers one's aggressive tendencies to surface on the road?

Anger and Aggression

Anger surely is a normal human emotion. The external expression of anger can range in intensity from impatient irritability to violent rage. For some, physiological conditions, such as chemical imbalances or psychological factors, contribute to its display. For others, environmental stressors come into play. Studies have suggested that people who are prone to anger are more likely to have strokes, need by-pass surgery or angioplasty, or die prematurely of cardiovascular disease than those who are not. They further state that stress hormones, such as adrenaline and cortisol, spur the system into action by triggering blood pressure and constricting blood vessels. Consequently, if you experience chronic anger, are "angry at the world," and harbor hostility and resentment, you may literally feel your "blood boiling." [32] Volumes have been written about the subject of anger, yet similar to mercury, anger is difficult to grasp and contain. Each person knows it, experiences it, and feels it, though for many it is difficult to manage. Anger is as common today as the toxic pollution wafting through the cities. It seems pervasive, evidenced at every turn of daily life. As with the cells that comprise bodily organs, anger is very much a part of everyone. Although anger is a component of everyone's structure, its impetus and expression is as different as each person's character pattern.

Though anger is expressed in a variety of ways, there are essentially two types of display, namely, overt or manifest anger, and covert or latently masked anger. Overt anger is direct, hostile, and aggressive, whereas, the other side of the anger coin, covert or masked anger, normally is suppressed to the point of repression. In the latter, one predictably withdraws from angry tirades, though at times may display passive-aggressive behaviors, while overt anger finds a direct target through its expression. With respect to anger-provoking situations, drivers experiencing overt anger tend to be irritable, resentful, and likely display outwardly aggressive behavior, while the drivers experiencing covert anger tend toward restraint, without displaying outwardly aggressive behavior. Yet, the latter, likely experience a greater degree anxiety in the trade-off.

Anger and aggression seemingly appear to be inextricably linked, though both are very distinct phenomena. Anger is an emotion, the affective aspect of consciousness or simply our internal feelings. Aggression, on the other hand, is a behavior—the way we conduct ourselves. Behaviors are controllable, while internal feelings are not. Aggressive behavior no doubt can kindle anger. Moreover, anger can help ignite aggressive behavior. In truth, on the road as in life, anger is legitimate, while aggression is not. Aggression is often undertaken simply to harm another through physical, psychological, or verbal abuse. "It is important to realize that the feeling of anger can serve as a useful warning sign that you are about to engage in aggressive or self-destructive behavior." [33] Anger alerts us that something is wrong and warns us to monitor impending aggressive behavioral threats.

Common aggressive behaviors include speeding, tailgating, cutting off other vehicles, running red lights, rude gestures, passing on the shoulder, and of course, driving under the influence of drugs and/or alcohol. Arguably, excessive speeding is responsible for many serious accidents and its practice is characteristic of *type-A* individuals. "Speeding—exceeding the posted limit or driving too fast for conditions—is one of the most prevalent factors contributing to traffic crashes." [34] Among the more than four hundred surveys examined, slightly more than 15% of the total sample generally drove faster than other drivers, with excessive speed inversely correlated to age. Poor impulse control is normally responsible for excessive speed and strongly associated with aggressive behavior.

Though certain behaviors are clearly identifiable as

aggressive, what actually precipitates one's aggression? To be sure, many factors contribute to one's anger arousal. Its physical and psychological arousal, serving as an adaptive response, is experienced by everyone. How one manages the anger and reacts, though, is a function of personality. Some can feel angry without expressing aggressive behavior. Others cannot. The adaptive, normal experience of anger, however, is fleeting and short-lived, while the maladaptive, abnormal experience lingers and is long lasting. Nevertheless, anger serves as a warning that protective behavior is necessary when the biological system is threatened. What, then, activates the body's automatic physiologic response? Coupled with anonymity on the road, the *invasion of one's personal space* triggers anger arousal with the potential for aggressive behavior. When others "invade" our personal space, anger alerts us to an impending threat and subsequently we adopt a fight or flight posture. We feel violated and ready ourselves for action. The impersonal anonymity we expect on the road quickly turns personal.

Personal Space

Personal space is a precious commodity guarded by all. In many large cities anonymity and crowding leads to alienation, not only on neighborhood streets, but also on the nation's highways, where drivers are simply nameless faces or robotic-like images steering the vehicle. Have you at times felt invisible like a non-person, simply motoring along through a sea of metal? Yet, does anonymity give someone a license to intrude upon another? If, for example, drivers view other motorists as non-persons by treating them as part of the invisible landscape, cannot privacy and personal space be more easily usurped? And so it is. It happens, often without notice. Shrouded in anonymity, anger is suddenly aroused when deprivation of personal space occurs, resulting in some form of aggressive behavior. On crowded highways, even with clear demarcated lanes, shouldn't the discretion of each driver ultimately delineate space territoriality? Therein lies the crux of the problem—how is one's personal space defined?

Several decades ago, Edward T. Hall introduced the word *proxemics*—the science of how our use of personal space affects us as well as its required parameters. He wrote, "It is in the nature of animals, including man, to exhibit behavior that we call territoriality."[35] Of course, the amount of space required and how it is defended depends on one's culture and personality. In driving, too, personality style dictates the emotional space required and maintained as well as the reaction to those who attempt to deprive us of our defined, yet indiscernible, area.

Americans respect and require personal, territorial space, according to Hall's study of *proxemics*. The four categories include, intimate, personal, social, and public, and varying ranges of distance are prescribed for each one.[36] Hall's proxemic classification system is significant, since "the specific distance chosen depends on the transaction; the relationship of the interacting individuals, how they feel, and what they are doing."[37] To violate these real, but imaginary areas of personal space is tantamount to impinging on one's "instinctive" rights. On a highway, for example, we may feel that personal space becomes limited when sandwiched between two semis, constrained by the insistent tailgater, or compressed by the motorist driving too slowly in the fast lane, with all "invasions" being cause for some degree of distress among motorists. Initially, feelings of discomfort engulf us, and thoughts naturally turn to devising a plan to extricate ourselves from this confining situation and quickly return to a desirable and comfortable space zone on the road. We are reminded by safety experts to maintain a proper vehicle distance to allow for adequate reaction time by adhering to the three-second (or four-second) rule. For example, if a vehicle is traveling at 55-mph, a one-second interval measures a distance of 81 feet, whereas the distance traveled in three seconds is 243 feet. When a careless and thoughtless driver wedges into our measured space that has been safely secured, we become emotionally unsettled if only for an instant with the intrusion of a stranger into our personal space.

As animals protect their territorial boundaries, humans likewise defend personal space. Though defense of our space is not usually overtly aggressive, when we have to surrender personal space on the road, we do not like it. The violation, however, ignites our anger. Reducing the violations of space will greatly serve to moderate anger as well as rage on the road. Regardless of motivations, when space is violated even in the slightest way, particularly on congested highways, tensions mount and drivers' darker sides inevitably emerge. How we react to this invasion essentially depends on the nature of personality. Parked in the recesses of the aggressive individual's mind is the "fight" mode, while the timid personality would likely choose "flight." Non-aggressive adaptive personalities exercise restraint, but aggressive types choose otherwise. Some motorists curb their anger, while others are driven to act out feelings of rage. Violation of personal space on the road remains a prominent trigger for aggressive behavior that ranges from mild irritation, such as mouthing a few angry words to violent road rage in its most severe form.

As mentioned throughout, how drivers actually respond to this invasion is essentially a function of one's personality driven by its hidden Hyde dimensions. As the drama unfolds on the road, the transformation, namely, the emergence of the "darker side" of one's personality, can surface spontaneously and without awareness. Recognizing the warning signs of our underlying personality structure when space-violation occurs is critical. Knowing and unmasking our "hidden Hyde" will ultimately lead us to adaptively script our driving performance.

Recognizing Mr. Hyde

Stevenson's *Dr. Jekyll and Mr. Hyde* examines the dual nature of the human person. He depicts both sides of our nature—the good, righteous demeanor individuals show to the outside world in the face of Jekyll and the masked aura of baseness, hidden from the world in the person of Hyde. In describing these two characters, Stevenson writes, "Even as good shone upon the countenance of the one, evil was written broadly and plainly on the face of the other. And yet when I looked upon that ugly idol in the glass, I was conscious of no repugnance, rather of a leap of welcome. This too was myself." [38]

The duality of Jekyll and Hyde coexists with varied characteristics of goodness and evil in the average person. Dr. Jekyll is a distinguished and respected scientist, who secretly maintains, if not relishes, the element of iniquity within him, though is unable to keep the darker, hidden side under control. In his youthful days, he had committed shameful indiscretions, yet as he grew old, he still yearned for the fun and frolic he enjoyed as a young man. As the story goes, Jekyll, after concocting and consuming the proper potion in his laboratory, was initially able to release the Hyde within him at will. Eventually, however, he realizes that it is exceedingly more difficult to control this part of him as time passes. Releasing this despicable side of him, he could without qualms of conscience enjoy the unencumbered, dark side of his transformed nature where Hyde is portrayed as a "bad little boy."

Stevenson's description of Mr. Hyde, a character we may find ourselves all too often imitating, confounds the Jekyll in us, particularly during times of stress when our internal defenses are weakened. Though we prefer to see ourselves as an upright Jekyll, demonstrating responsible, caring, and courteous behavior much of the time, Hyde's cruel, unsympathetic, and self-centered behaviors, on occasion, surreptitiously overwhelm the adaptive nature in all of us. What Stevenson reinforces is that there is a Hyde in everyone—the underlying shadow—hidden much deeper in those who are unmindful of its presence.

Jekyll could not easily reject the evil part of himself, though he struggled to do so. This often is the case for those who fail to become familiar with their own dark sides. Without warning and at times without conscious awareness, aggressive instincts overwhelm us. Nevertheless, it is at such times that the hidden Hyde is uncovered. "He would normally go to sleep as Henry Jekyll and wake up as Edward Hyde. We find him raging and freezing with the passions of Hyde."

Unfortunately, there are times when the hidden part, or the shadow—the Hyde character—finds dramatic expression in the normal, adaptive personality. As the name implies, Hyde is the part of Jekyll that was hidden—or hides—from society. The name of the character Jekyll was cleverly selected by Stevenson, as it refers to the French word *Je,* meaning I, and thus stands for "I kill." Dr. Jekyll, in effect, wants to kill the evil, disruptive side of himself. In the end, he discovers that the only means of killing this part of him is to kill the whole person. All along, Jekyll believes that he could control this dark side of himself, but eventually, without sufficient restraint, it overpowers him. Jekyll could not easily reject the dark side of himself, though he struggles to do so. When he looks in the mirror, he is unable to see the grotesque figure everyone else sees. Eventually, he concludes, "Good and evil shift from face to face."

What causes people to act out, transforming them from a Jekyll into a Hyde? Could it possibly be a dormant quality of their personality suddenly surfacing? Vulnerability is a by-product of stress, with various personalities responding differently. Negativity creeps into the mind, and our normal controls seemingly become unhinged. Sometimes, though, the anger can be checked, as we question what had come over us, and regain control over our emotions. Nevertheless, all too often, the demons seem to be released and, as a result, control is lost.

There may have been a time when you experienced a sudden outburst of rage that suddenly seemed out of character. You quickly catch yourself, but then question perplexedly, "Why did I do that?" This is predictably an instance of your shadow "acting up," so to speak

To understand the answer more thoroughly, you must search the depths of the unconscious. William Booth, in his introduction to Robert Bly's [39] book about the *Shadow*, notes that the shadow is a long bag that individuals drag behind, "heavy with the parts of ourselves our parents or community didn't approve of." Bly implies that you spend the first 20 years deciding what parts of yourself to stuff into the bag, and spend the rest of your life trying to get them out again in discovering who your true self is. He says that later in life, fear is elicited when the bag is opened. Inside this bag, the shadow elements contain aspects of yourself that you can't accept. The experience is too painful to feel. Without warning, and at times without conscious awareness, aggressive instincts become overwhelming because the shadow feels the rage of years of containment. It is then you realize the weight of the bag. How often did you say or do something, only to later admit that you didn't mean to say or do it? Bly would insist that the shadow represents all that is instinctive in you. Unfortunately, when you get glimpses of these underdeveloped and buried aspects of yourself, their very existence is fearfully denied. The baser qualities, as those of Mr. Hyde, are deeply pressed into your unconscious, far out from view of your conscious self. Yet, these aspects are very active in life and cause consternation if your bag is not open or its contents sorted through. As Toub [40] advises, "One of the major ways to integrate our inner opposites is by consciously confronting the shadow—the dark part of the personality that contains the undesirable qualities and attributes we refuse to own." As was Dr. Jekyll's mistake, many attempt to escape the tension within rather than embracing the duality that exists. With reference to projecting the shadow, Wilber writes, "Like the projection of negative emotions, the projection of negative qualities is very common in our society, for we have been duped into equating 'negative' with 'undesirable.' Thus instead of befriending and integrating our negative traits, we alienate and project them, seeing them in everybody else but ourselves."[41] Only through embracing your shadow, can it be unmasked. "Know thyself" read the inscription over the portal of the 6th century BC Greek temple of Apollo at Delphi. Masks simply disguise our real selves. "Meeting the shadow calls for slowing the pace of life, listening to the body's cues, and allowing ourselves time to be alone in order to digest the cryptic messages from the hidden world." [42] Retrieving the elusive part of your mind is the crux of the matter, for only the shadow knows.

In Summary

As discussed throughout the previous chapters, certain personality patterns have a greater proclivity to act aggressively. Aggression is the result of frustration, and its behavioral effects vary with each personality. Yet, the aggressive behaviors, which are all too common on our roads today, arguably, are symptoms of underlying hostility. The violation of personal space, inextricably linked to a driver's expression of rage on the road, unleashes our underlying hostility. The transformation from the adaptive Dr. Jekyll to the maladaptive Mr. Hyde then occurs. Hidden, like Hyde behind the cloak of Jekyll, the unconscious directs one's aggression on the road. As Robert Bly writes, "We notice that when sunlight hits the body, the body turns bright, but it throws a shadow, which is dark.

The brighter the light, the darker the shadow. Each of us has some part of our personality that is hidden from us." [43] Recognizing our hidden shadow will not only help to unmask aggressive impulses that drive us on the road, but will also define our true personality.

According to Shakespeare, *"All the world's a stage,"* and it is upon this stage where we come to know our true selves. As with actors on a stage, the more we perfect the masks we comfortably wear, the more deeply our dark sides remain hidden, and the more susceptible we become to the appearance of Mr. Hyde. Personality ultimately dictates our real aggressiveness on the road, uncovering the hidden Hyde in all of us. Unmasking these hidden impulses will provide the insight required to tame them. Given the various masks we wear on the stage of life, it is our performance on the road that defines who we are, leading to a clearer understanding of how "your personality drives you."

Endnotes

Preface

[1] *Emotions Profile Index* (EPI), Western Psychological Services.

Chapter One

2 Illinois Online Traffic Safety (2011). *trafficschool@northwestern.edu.*
3 *Ibid.*
[4] Original story by Frances Ann Burns Birmingham, Ala. (APBnews.com, Nov. 14, 2000).
[5] Figures illustrated throughout chapters two through nine include measurement data derived by using the basic dimensions in the *Emotions Profile Index* (EPI), Western Psychological Services. Since the EPI provides an accurate measure for the eight basic emotional dimensions developed by Plutchik and Kellerman, discussion of the various driving styles employed the EPI emotional dimensions as a basis of reference to arrive at the authors' interpretation of each driving style.

Chapter Two

[6] Source: JHuggins@JamesSHuggins.com.
[7] Millon and Everly (1985), p.33.
[8] Source: © Rozlyn Marshall "Roztopia" by Happy Gilmore.

Chapter Three

[9] David Shapiro, Neurotic Styles, (New York: Harper, 1965).
[10] Ibid.

Chapter Four

[11] Source:http://www.deerbrook.com/auto_safety/road_rage/10_tip s_o courteous driving.asp Copyright 2001.

Chapter Five

[12] Source: http://www.virtualvoyage.com/soapbox/sandy.htm.

Chapter Six

[13] McEvoy, S.P. et al.,(2005). British Medical Journal, 331:438.
[14] Strayer, D.L. et al., (2006). A Comparison of the Cell Phone Driver and the Drunk Driver. University of Utah.
[15] Lionells (1984).

Chapter Seven

[16] Millon and Davis, Disorders of Personality DSM-IV and Beyond, (1994).
[17] Ibid.
[18] Lesse (1979).
[19] NIH (2000).
[20] NHTSA/FARS, 2008.
[21] Lam, L.T. et al., (2005).Suicidal Ideation, Antidepressant Medication, and Car Crash Injury. Accident and Analysis Prevention, 37(2), 335-39.
[22] Joseph Wolpe.

Chapter Eight

[23] http://www.innovationgame.com/vedens/drivers.htm.

Chapter Nine

[24] Millon and Everly (1985), p.195.
[25] Millon (1985, p.200).
[26] Millon (1985), p. 200.
[27] Mahler (1935).
[28] Ibid.
[29] American Psychiatric Association. (1994). DSM-IV, Washington, DC; American Psychiatric Association.
[30] Source: HostileTimes.com ; (Names provided in the article were not included).
[31] Archives of General Psychiatry. (June, 2006).

Chapter Ten

[32] Harvard Heart Health Letter, (2004).
[33] Smith, J.C. (1993) Creative Stress Management. New Jersey: Prentice Hall.
[34] NHTSA (2008).
[35] Hall. ET, *The Hidden Dimension* (p.128, 1966).
[36] Ibid. (p.114).
[37] Ibid. (p.128).
[38] SparkNotes Editors. "SparkNote on Dr. Jekyll and Mr. Hyde." SparkNotes.com. SparkNotes LLC. 2003. Web. 4 Feb. 2011.
[39] Bly, R. , Little Book on the Human Shadow (p.2, 1988).
[40] Zweig, C. & Abrams, J. (1991), Meeting the Shadow.: Hidden
[41] Power of the Dark Side of Human Nature, p. 253.
Ibid. (p. 273).
[42] Ibid. (p. xix).
[43] Bly, R., Little Book on the Human Shadow (p.7, 1988).

About the Author

Dan Jankowski, PsyD, earned his doctorate in clinical psychology at the Illinois School for Professional Psychology. Among his appointments, Dr. Jankowski taught Objective Personality Assessment and Stress Management as adjunct professor at Roosevelt University. Currently he is in private practice, devoting the majority of his time to research and writing. He is the author of *A Beginner's Guide to the MCMI-III*, published by the American Psychological Association.

Notes:

www.ingramcontent.com/pod-product-compliance
Lightning Source LLC
Chambersburg PA
CBHW072127280526
45788CB00002B/578